BOUTIQUE ICECREAM

LIBERATING
THE WORLD ONE LICK AT A TIME

THE ICECREAMISTS®

AGENTS OF COOL

ICE CREAM IS EXQUISITE. WHAT A PITY IT IS NOT ILLEGAL. VOLTAIRE

First published in Great Britain
in 2012 by Mitchell Beazley, an imprint of Octopus
Publishing Group Limited, Endeavour House, 189 Shaftesbury
Avenue, London, WC2H 8JY www.octopusbooks.co.uk

An Hachette UK Company
www.hachette.co.uk

Design and Layout copyright © Octopus Publishing Group Ltd 2012
Text copyright © Matt O'Connor 2012
www.theicecreamists.com

978-1-84533-706-3

A CIP record for this book is available from the British Library.

Set in Quadraat, Trajan, Monster Days and Drunken Shower.

Printed and bound in China.

Commissioning Editor: Eleanor Maxfield | Art Direction & Design: Yasia Williams-Leedham
Photography: Anders Schonnemann | Home Economist: Laura Fyfe
Props Styling: Rachel Jukes | Production: Caroline Alberti
Editor: Jo Wilson | Copy Editor: Patricia Burgess
Proofreader: Kate Fox | Indexer: Hilary Bird

Note: Some recipes contain nuts and nut derivatives. Anyone with a known
nut allergy must avoid these. This book contains some dishes made with
raw or lightly cooked eggs. It is prudent for more vulnerable people
such as pregnant and nursing mothers, invalids, the elderly, babies
and young children, to avoid raw or lightly cooked eggs.

Contents

INTRODUCTION: THE SCOOP, THE WHOLE SCOOP AND NOTHING BUT THE SCOOP

There is nothing more incongruous than the collision of unforeseen and spectacular life-changing events that led to the creation of The Icecreamists. It began when I was an excitable, stuttering, five-year-old seaside boy, waiting for my father to buy me my first-ever Flake 99 ice cream as I gripped a stick of rock in one hand and a Kiss Me Quick hat in the other.

We lived on what we affectionately called 'Planet Thanet', a piece of chalky rock bobbing around at the southern end of the North Sea, surrounded by the crumbling seaside towns of Margate, Ramsgate and Broadstairs. As I left the ice cream parlour on Margate seafront, I used the chocolate Flake bar to press the ice cream gently down into the cone to make sure every mouthful consisted of softly whipped ice cream and crunchy wafer pieces.

But I was then to experience for the first time the bittersweet pain of loss as, juggling my stick of rock and hat, I dropped my frozen treat on to the seafront. My father couldn't help but laugh as I stood weeping, ice cream dripping down my T-shirt and melting into the pores of the concrete promenade. The sadness and humour in what that dropped ice cream represented remains with me to this day: a reminder that, like childhood, life passes all too soon; innocence lost, melting away in a decaying seaside town.

From that early age my fascination with ice cream was not only enduring, but became a metaphor for life: it was fickle, fleeting, fragile and in a permanent state of flux. It is no exaggeration to say it would shape my life emotionally, physically and politically.

After I escaped from Planet Thanet, there followed a 20-year career in ice cream as a consultant for the likes of Unilever and Mars, before becoming creative director on major UK ice cream brands and launching the UK's first Italian gelato, 'Antonio Federici'.

Even when I faced profound personal challenges after losing contact with my children during a painful divorce, I found solace and inspiration in the cold comfort of ice cream.

NOTHING ELSE ON GOD'S EARTH CONNECTED ME TO MY INNER CHILD LIKE THE MEMORY OF MY FIRST FLAKE 99

I was the same excitable five year-old boy from Planet Thanet, but trapped in the body of a 40-year-old man.

ICECREAMIST: A PERSON ADDICTED TO OR OBSESSED WITH ICE CREAM. *'AN EXTREME ICE CREAM FANATIC.'* ICECREAMISM CAN BE HIGHLY ADDICTIVE AND INFECTIOUS.

In 2008 I persuaded my family to join me on my deranged adventure with some research trips, first to New York, and then to the beguiling, jewel-encrusted coves of the Italian riviera and the shimmering ports of Portofino and Rapallo. From there, I studied with Italian gelato master Roberto Lobrano and realized that whilst Italian gelato was the Holy Grail for an ice cream evangelist like me, it was bound by a frustratingly rigid set of Italian traditions and codes. As I pursued the idea of an experimental ice cream concept, I found a whole plethora of facts that would seed the idea in my head, of ice cream as a medium for political protest.

To my mind, it could be elevated to another level by cold-fusing it with cocktail techniques and pop culture influences to create ice cream from another dimension. Of course, this was heresy to many of my Italian colleagues, but Roberto rose to the challenge, producing sublime gelatos that transported artisan ice cream to vertiginous new heights.

I then tapped into my melting pot of other influences, cross-fertilizing ideas from abstract reference points with a team of chefs and cocktail mixologists. We put ice cream on toast, added popping candy that would blow your fillings out, we blowtorched ice cream at the table, flamed another with a shot of 90% home-made chilli vodka – all in an attempt to satiate my pyromaniac tendencies.

The final chapter in the development of the whipped-up, mixed-up, upside-down world of The Icecreamists was shaped in the various custody suites and police cells I holidayed in during my campaigning days. As the founder of Fathers 4 Justice, I had a background in staging dramatic, high-profile events that explored the outer extremities of the law and breached national security with alarming frequency – much to the chagrin of the British government.

This coincided with a fashionably brief stint in rehab, where I concluded that ice cream had previously unrealized addictive and hallucinatory properties. The idea of 'icecreamism' was born in a *One Flew Over the Cuckoo's Nest* moment as I challenged patients to 'lick their addiction' with Randle P. McMurphy gusto. 'Take me to my dealer!' I would announce to the nursing staff as I berated my Librium-popping chums for their over-enthusiastic consumption of drugs designed to knock them into a catatonic stupor.

I CONCLUDED THERE AND THEN, THERE COULD BE NO BETTER MEDIUM THAN ICE CREAM TO CELEBRATE THE CULTURE OF ADDICTION

In June 2008 I had retired from frontline campaigning to devote the next few years of my life to this as yet unnamed ice cream project. Scotland Yard, concerned that my move into ice cream might be some elaborate cover story for the overthrow of the British government (I jest not), sent two officers from Counter Terrorism Command down to Romsey in Hampshire, where I was living at the time. As I was being questioned inquisitorially about the authenticity of my love of ice cream, they told me of their concern about 'domestic extremists'. I fixed my icy gaze on the senior officer and flippantly declared, 'I am not an extremist, I am an icecreamist.' And there, in that moment of absurdity, sitting in front of counter terrorism police officers, The Icecreamists were born.

My next mission would be to liberate the world — one lick at a time

BRAIN FREEZE

THE HISTORY OF ICE CREAM IS PLAGUED with inaccurate and often fabricated claims. Early evidence of ice cream comes from China between 618 and 907, during the Tang period. King Shang used to have a frozen dish made for him out of buffalo milk, flour and camphor.

GELATO is credited to Bernardo Buontalenti, a 16th-century Florentine, who presented his creation to the court of Catherina de Medici. However, this is disputed, as variations of gelato are thought to have existed in many similar forms for thousands of years.

THE WORLD'S TOP FIVE consumers of ice cream per capita are the USA, New Zealand, Denmark, Australia and Belgium.

THE COLDER IT GETS the more ice cream you eat. The highest consumption of ice cream per capita in Europe is in chilly Scandinavia.

ICE CREAM SUNDAES were created when in the late 19th century when it was illegal to sell ice cream with flavoured soda on a Sunday in the American town of Evanston. Traders circumnavigated the law by serving ice cream with a syrup and calling it an 'Ice Cream Sunday'. They later replaced the 'y' with an 'e' to avoid upsetting religious leaders.

CAN YOU LICK IT? Yes you can! American presidents have a long association with ice cream. As a boy, President 'Ike' Eisenhower worked as a boy in the ice cream factory of the Belle Springs Creamery Company in Abilene, Kansas. During the 1960 American presidential election, voters could choose between the Nixon Bar and the Kennedy Bar, both of which carried pictures of the candidates. President Barack Obama used to work for Baskin Robbins, an American Ice Cream brand.

RIVAL GANGS in Glasgow during the 1980s used ice cream vans as a cover for selling drugs and stolen goods, resulting in the infamous 'Glasgow Ice Cream Wars'. Strathclyde Police were later nicknamed the 'Serious Chimes Squad' for their alleged incompetence in dealing with the gang warfare.

IN THE FORMER SOVIET REPUBLIC OF BELARUS 'Organized ice cream eating' was banned by the president because it was considered an unauthorized public assembly. Government agents broke up the event, arresting many of the people the government regarded as 'extremists'. The idea of organized ice cream eating as political protest was born.

BAGHDAD enjoyed more ice cream per capita head during the Iraq War than the Americans did in some US cities.

IN THE 2008 GAZA WAR the Israelis bombed the Al Ameer ice cream factory in Gaza. Owner Yaser Alwadeya said, 'I can't figure out why the Israelis thought that Hamas had anything to do with ice cream.'

DURING PROHIBITION major breweries, including Anheuser-Busch and Stroh's, produced barrels of ice cream instead of spirits.

ADOLF HITLER decreed in July 1933 that German ice cream had to contain at least 10% milk-fat.

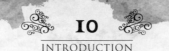
One small lick for man. One giant scoop for mankind

In 2009, as the world was in economic meltdown, The Icecreamists were about to occupy 3,500 square feet of Selfridges department store, London, with a subterranean God Save the Cream guerrilla-punk pop-up boutique. This was no ordinary ice cream parlour, rather a deliciously twisted satanic temple of cool filtered through my febrile imagination. Selfridges rocked to our house band (called, naturally, The Icecreamists), there was a cinema and we also had an ice cream van covered in political slogans and driven by a dummy of Her Majesty the Queen.

The boutique also dispensed our first infamous ice cream cocktail, The Sex Pistol. This frisky little minx consisted of 'natural stimulant' ice cream and a shot of absinthe served from an intravenous drip by Nurse Selena. Not only was this medication that needed administering, but when we put it in a cone, a national newspaper dubbed it the 'Whorenetto'. This was an ice cream with enough erectile properties to raise people from the dead.

But the stimulant ice cream also aroused vast amounts of press attention and controversy. Within days it was 'Sex Pistols at dawn', as the punk band I had mistakenly assumed to be dead turned out to be alive and claiming that our ice cream infringed their intellectual copyright of the Queen. I pointed out that our use of the Queen was subverting their subversion of the Queen's image, which they didn't have permission to use in the first place.

We arrived in London's Covent Garden in February 2011 with the snarling, schizophrenic mash-up of apocalyptic cool that was our first permanent store. We opened with a 'Lick Your Addiction' treatment programme of sub-zero elixirs that had been specifically tailored to treat lapsed hell-raisers, recovering hedonists and practising satirists, fugitives and diabetics. It was then that my long-suffering benefactor and business partner, the incomparable Frank Frederick, challenged me to create an ice cream story in the middle of winter that would end up on CNN.

I dutifully consulted my vault of recipes and concepts and resurrected the idea of breast milk ice cream.

SOME PEOPLE ARGUED AGAINST THE IDEA, SAYING THAT BREAST MILK WAS A BODILY FLUID, 'BUT SO IS COWS' MILK,' I REPLIED. 'BREAST MILK IS FOR KIDS,' SAID OTHERS. 'WELL, GUESS WHAT?' I RESPONDED. 'COWS' MILK IS FOR CALVES.'

WHATEVER IS FUNNY IS SUBVERSIVE. EVERY JOKE IS A CUSTARD PIE. A DIRTY JOKE A SORT OF MENTAL REBELLION. GEORGE ORWELL

Human beings, I had discovered, are the only mammals that drink the milk of other mammals. I was fascinated by society's revulsion to breast milk. This was an opportunity for a taboo-breaking, iconoclastic ice cream.

So it happened. We called it Baby Gaga and advertised for donors on Mumsnet. Fifteen came forward, but I chose mother of one Victoria Hiley. She was an articulate exponent of breast-feeding. She was screened in line with hospital standards and we went ahead and made our first batch. On 25 February 2011 we opened our doors to what became a global phenomenon.

For added satirical authenticity, we said the ice cream was freshly squeezed, free range and totally natural, and came served with a shot of Calpol and a baby teething biscuit. An added bonus was that it was also suitable for anyone who was lactose intolerant.

We sold out of Baby Gaga ice cream within the first hour. By the second hour the world's press had descended on our humble emporium. By the evening we'd been busted by the food fascists from Westminster Council (now dubbed Breastminster Council), who marched in as if they were looking for bio-hazardous chemical waste, seized two remaining scoops left for the press and banned Baby Gaga ice cream. As they left, I endeavoured to point out that whilst you could drink and smoke yourself to death in the London Borough of Westminster, there had never been a single recorded death in the history of humanity from the consumption of human breast milk. The fact that breast milk had weaned the world seemed to have escaped them. We responded by placing posters in the window: 'Frozen out by Nanny State'.

The following Monday the media storm continued and I attracted attention from an outraged pop-megastar Lady Gaga. She declared that Baby Gaga was an infringement of her name and that the ice cream was both 'provocative and nausea-inducing'.

We now had over 300 breast-milk donors and could have opened a milking parlour instead of an ice cream parlour. Westminster Council admitted they had 'boobed' and gave Baby Gaga a clean bill of health, and Lady Gaga eventually realized that the more she threatened us, the more publicity we got.

After repelling the threat of both closure and bankruptcy, we opened our second store in the Piazza, Covent Garden, about a month later. After 40 years, the story of The Icecreamists was complete.

Today The Icecreamists are shaping a new world of oral gratification with a decadent kaleidoscope of mind-altering icescapades in cold fused refreshments. We remain a theatrically minded troupe of provocateurs and cold warriors, hopelessly foul-mouthed, anti-Establishment and politically incorrect. But we have purged ourselves of our old law-breaking ways and dedicated our lives to converting a cold, cruel, unforgiving world to the life-enhancing gospel of freshly made artisan gelato.

WE SAY ICECREAMISM IS A BIT LIKE CAPITALISM OR SOCIALISM, ONLY FUNNIER, MORE ADDICTIVE AND BETTER TASTING

You can enjoy it against a bar, against the wall or against the law.

This is the inside scoop on The Icecreamists. Join me on my mission to boldly go where no ice cream brand has gone before. To liberate the world one lick at a time.

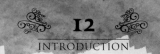
FORGIVE ME, FATHER, FOR I HAVE SINNED

THIS ISN'T YOUR NORMAL RECIPE BOOK – THIS IS PART ICE CREAM BIBLE, PART CONFESSIONAL

Over the years many people have asked me why they should make their own ice creams and sorbettos when they can buy 'luxury' ice cream or sorbet from any corner shop. As an ice cream evangelist, I am naturally biased, but there are a few simple reasons.

First, most so-called luxury ice cream is very high in fat and sugar, and uses a variety of stabilizers and emulsifiers for a long shelf life. The fat masks the flavour of the ice cream, and the other inclusions often cover up the fact that the ice cream itself isn't actually very good. Likewise, store-bought sorbets are often more colourings and concentrates than real fruit. You can make your own delicious organic alternatives at a fraction of the price you buy it in the shop.

Second, nothing can compare to the epiphany you will experience when making fresh ice cream and creating your own flavours. Most bog-standard ice cream is made with vegetable fat and hasn't seen a cow in its life. The only thing manufacturers are milking is you, not the bovine. Your relationship with ice cream should be akin to an enduring and dangerous infatuation with a beautiful member of the opposite sex – bewitching, intoxicating and potentially deadly.

Our boutique ice cream mixes are variations on traditional Italian gelato and are made with a slightly higher fat content for a richer mouthfeel. The strange, sub-zero alchemy we use to blend full-fat milk, double cream and egg yolks is the foundation for most of our recipes. Our sorbettos, or water-ices, are made from a traditional Italian sugary syrupy base.

SO YOU WANT TO BE AN ICECREAMIST...?

CHOOSE YOUR POISON

You'll find recipes for delicious boutique ice creams and sorbettos for you to master in chapters 1 and 2.

ARM YOURSELF

Decide whether you are making by machine or hand (See pages 14–15).

LOCK AND LOAD

Get tips on tools and ingredients, plus a troubleshooting section (see page 157).

DISCOVER YOUR VICE

Once you've mastered the basic ice creams and sorbettos, you can tackle vice cream cocktails, icequakes, sundaes, desserts and lollies in chapters 3, 4 and 5.

DEVIATE FROM THE SYSTEM

 This symbol tells you what delicious variations the featured ice cream or sorbetto is used in. So if you've made A Chocwork Orange ice cream on page 28, you can use it in the Fire and Vice cocktail on page 114.

FIND YOUR MOTHER ICE CREAM

 This symbol shows which basic ice cream recipe you'll need to whip up a concoction. So if you like the look of Nuclear Winter ice cream sundae on page 136 you'll need to use Priscilla Cream of the Dessert on page 22.

THE ALCHEMY OF ICE CREAM

CHOOSE ME

Choose your recipe and prepare the basic mix at least 12–24 hours ahead of churning the finished ice cream. The mix will take no longer than 20 minutes to put together.

SIZE ME UP

The amount made by each recipe varies slightly, depending on what extra ingredients are added to the base mix.

Most machines will make about 850ml (1½ pints) of ice cream, though we recommend making 500ml (17fl oz) quantities because the ice cream expands as the air is churned in, and the machine can struggle if it is filled to the maximum. Also the more mix you put in the machine, the slower the mix will freeze.

Iffyou have a large machine or want to make large batches of ice cream, simply multiply the quantities according to the size of the batch you require. Just make sure you've got enough space in your refrigerator for the mix.

TEMPER ME

An ice cream base is composed of heated milk and cream, combined with whisked eggs and sugar. When you pour the hot milk and cream mix on to the egg and sugar mix, do so gradually and slowly whilst whisking continuously to temper the eggs and prevent them from scrambling.

The mix should be heated to no more than 85°C (185°F), or until you can see bubbles – about 5 minutes.

CHILL ME

When the mix is ready, pour into a heatproof bowl and set aside for about 30 minutes, stirring occasionally, until cooled to room temperature. For more rapid chilling, place the bowl in a sink half-filled with water and some ice for 20 minutes. Don't put the base mix directly in the refrigerator.

When cooled, cover the mix and refrigerate, ideally overnight, but at least for 6 hours, until thoroughly chilled to at least 4°C (39°F).

WHIP ME

An ice cream machine isn't essential, but we do recommend having one. The results from a good ice cream machine are often so gob-smackingly delicious that they will nearly always surpass your expectations in terms of flavour and mouthfeel.

A machine will make your life easier and the whole process a lot more fun. More importantly, it will pay for itself over and over again. For further information on specific models see page 156.

Churning will take about 20–60 minutes, depending on your machine and how cold the mix is. Always follow the manufacturer's instructions.

BEAT ME

Making ice cream by hand is a traditional and low-cost approach, but it's a lengthy process, and freezing a liquid base mix into a solid can create nasty hard ice crystals that compromise the smooth and creamy mouthfeel you are trying to achieve. A good stick blender or electric whisk will make the experience infinitely less demanding. However, should you crave a full cardiac workout to offset diabetes, give hand-whisking a whirl.

1. Select a recipe from the book and prepare the mix according to the recipe.

2. Chill as instructed, then pour the mixture into a plastic container, cover with a lid and place in your freezer for 50 minutes.

3. Remove from the freezer and beat with an electric whisk or stick blender to remove any ice crystals. Return to the freezer.

4. Over the next 2–3 hours, remove from the freezer every 30 minutes or so and whisk or beat again. Finally leave until completely frozen.

SERVE ME

Delivering the perfect serve is a delicate balancing act. Too cold and the ice cream will be difficult to scoop; too soft and it will melt too quickly. If your ice cream is hard to the touch, leave it at room temperature for around 5 minutes, or until soft enough to scoop. As with sex, timing is everything!

LICK ME, SUCK ME

When you are making ice cream, it's the flavours that matter, not the colour. You should continually taste your mix (using a clean teaspoon) when it is warm and after freezing to ensure you are happy with the flavour. All your ice creams will be a natural, pastel hue. The bright colours you often see in ice cream parlours are achieved by using artificial colourants.

LICK ME QUICK

If you are up against the clock, here is a handy method for making ice cream quickly.

1. Chill the mix as described in step 2 (Beat me).

2. Place the bowl in your freezer on a 'super-freeze' setting if you have one and leave for 30 minutes, or until the mixture is cold to the touch, stirring occasionally.

3. Pour into an ice cream machine and churn according to the manufacturer's instructions.

4. Once churned pour into a plastic container with a lid and place in the lowest part of your freezer for at least 1½ hours to set.

5. Enjoy!

TEN COMMANDMENTS OF COOL

1. THOU SHALT FOLLOW THE COMMANDMENTS

We encourage you to start with our basic boutique ice cream recipes – what we call our Twisted Classics – religiously until you get them just right. After that you can deviate from the recipes (and we always encourage deviation at The Icecreamists). During the flavouring and freezing processes you will be able to conjure up other flavours with miraculous simplicity and flair.

2. THOU SHALT NOT BE INTIMIDATED BY THE GORGEOUS PHOTOGRAPHY

This book is idiot-proof. How do I know? It was road-tested on me. Many years ago, when I went to make my first batch of ice cream, I stood looking at my brand new machine and complained to my wife that it looked 'absolutely filthy'. She shot me a withering look and told me it was our old breadmaker. If I can make a career out of ice cream after that, you can surely make great ice cream.

3. THOU SHALT FREEZE YOUR ASSETS

Keep everything – milk, cream, ice cream mix, fruit and other ingredients – super-chilled in your fridge. This will assist during the production process and help give your ice cream the smooth, luxurious mouthfeel you desire. If you have space, keep your whisks and mixing bowls in the fridge too, or at the very least in the coolest part of your house. You can also chill the plastic container.

4. THOU SHALT NEVER COMPROMISE ON INGREDIENTS

The quality of the ingredients you use will have a direct impact on the flavour of your ice cream. Always use seasonal produce whenever possible, especially when choosing fruit for sorbettos. Do not short-change your ice cream by using artificial sweeteners, low-fat milks and suchlike (see page 155). Boutique ice cream already has less fat than standard ice cream, and it needs that fat to create texture and mouthfeel, and to prevent the mix from developing ice crystals. Moral of the story: if you want to be a choirboy, go to church instead.

5. THOU SHALT LEARN THE ART OF PATIENCE

The history of ice cream production is shrouded in historical code, mystery, superstition and tradition. The real trick is learning the art of patience. You have to make your mix, then chill it, probably overnight, churn it in an ice cream machine and freeze it for a few hours – all that even if you are only making as little as half a litre. But it's an ice cream that's been made with a whole lotta love. The joy of making your own is a pleasure you can't measure or put a price on.

6. THOU SHALT ENJOY ON THE SAME DAY

The ice creams in this book will keep for up to a week in the freezer, but all homemade ice creams are best enjoyed straightway, as the longer they are kept, the icier they will become. Super-fresh ice cream is the ultimate indulgence.

7. THOU SHALT ALLOW TO SOFTEN

Every ice maiden should have a soft and scoopable centre lying under her permafrost exterior. Always leave your ice cream to soften for at least 5 minutes at room temperature so it is served at the right consistency. This will also help when scooping.

8. THOU SHALT NEVER REFREEZE

Never refreeze or consume ice cream once it has melted. This is what's known in the trade as 'temperature abuse'. The ice cream will taste gritty, like a mouthful of penguin droppings. You have been warned.

9. THOU SHALT LICK YOUR BOWL CLEAN

The ultimate sign of customer satisfaction is when my six-year-old son Archie is holding up the ice-cream bowl to his face, drinking the creamy dregs. This might not meet most people's idea of table etiquette, but in the world of The Icecreamists, you have permission to lick your bowl. In fact, we would consider it rude not to.

10. THOU SHALT PREPARE YOUR NEXT RECIPE

Now you have accepted your challenge to become an icecreamist, the rules of engagement are as follows: ice cream is not a spectator sport – it's a religion. Get whipping.

BOUTI

QUE *ice creams*

YOUR MISSION, SHOULD YOU CHOOSE TO ACCEPT IT, IS TO CREATE A MIND-ALTERING KALEIDOSCOPE OF VICE CREAMS AND OTHER GUILTY PLEASURES WHILST SAFELY ENSCONCED IN THE BOSOM OF YOUR OWN KITCHEN. FOR PURVEYORS OF ORAL GRATIFICATION, WHAT BETTER PLACE TO START THAN SOME SIMPLE TWISTED CLASSICS? NEXT MOVE ON TO OUR NOTORIOUS AND LOVEABLE ROGUES & ECCENTRICS, AND GET CARRIED AWAY WITH SOME DIET-BUSTING GUILTY PLEASURES FOLLOWED BY SOME SPIKED CREAMS. FINALLY, WHEN YOUR MISSION IS ACCOMPLISHED AND YOU SUCCUMB TO THE INFECTIOUS SYMPTOMS OF 'ICECREAMISM', PLEDGE YOUR ALLEGIANCE WITH THE WORDS 'GOD SAVE THE CREAM'."

NOTE: ALL THE RECIPES IN THIS CHAPTER TAKE 20 MINUTES TO PREPARE THE BASE MIX OR CUSTARD, 6–24 HOURS FOR CHILLING, AND 20–60 MINUTES FOR CHURNING. ALL RECIPES MAKE JUST OVER 500ML (17FL OZ), WHICH WILL SERVE FOUR PEOPLE, AND ARE BEST ENJOYED WITHIN A FEW DAYS OF MAKING.

THE VANILLA MONOLOGUES

MADAGASCAN VANILLA ICE CREAM

THIS IS THE MOTHER OF ALL MELTDOWNS – THE ICE CREAM THAT SETS THE BENCHMARK FOR EVERY OTHER IN THIS BOOK. THIS SUB-ZERO CLASSIC WILL LEAVE YOU MONOLOGUING FOR HOURS. A GREAT VANILLA ICE CREAM MADE WITH SOUL THAT GOES STRAIGHT TO THE HEART.

• 250ml (8fl oz) full-fat milk • 125ml (4fl oz) double cream • 1 fat vanilla pod, split lengthways • 2 egg yolks • 88g (3¼oz) caster sugar • pinch of sea salt

1. Pour the milk and cream into a large saucepan. Scrape in the vanilla seeds, then add the empty pod and heat gently, stirring occasionally, until the mixture begins to steam but not boil.

2. Meanwhile, whisk the egg yolks in a heatproof bowl until smooth. Add the sugar and salt and whisk until pale and slightly fluffy. Gradually and slowly, pour the hot milk into the egg mixture whilst whisking continuously to prevent the eggs scrambling. Return the mixture to the saucepan and place over a low heat, stirring frequently until the custard thinly coats the back of a wooden spoon. Do not allow to boil.

3. Pour back into the bowl and set aside for about 30 minutes, stirring occasionally, until cooled to room temperature. For more rapid chilling, half-fill a sink with cold water and ice and place the bowl of mixture in it for 20 minutes. Never put the hot mixture into the fridge.

4. Once cooled, cover the mixture and refrigerate, ideally overnight, but at least for 6 hours, until thoroughly chilled (at least 4°C).

5. Remove the vanilla pod and pour the mixture into an ice cream machine. Churn according to the manufacturer's instructions. If making by hand, see the instructions on page 15.

6. When the churning is completed, use a spoon or spatula to scrape the ice cream into a freezer-proof container with a lid (to protect the ice cream from surface frosting in the freezer). Freeze until it reaches the correct scooping texture (at least 2 hours). You can rinse and dry vanilla pods after use, then store them in sugar or use them for future ice-cream-making or baking.

MY SEX IS ICE CREAM MARILYN MONROE

A RICH, LUXURIOUS BLEND OF FRESH CREAM INFUSED WITH EXOTIC BLACK PEARLS
FROM THE MADAGASCAN VANILLA POD

Inside scoop

USED IN ≫ THE CRYBABY PG 110

PRISCILLA CREAM OF THE DESSERT

WHITE CHOCOLATE ICE CREAM

INSPIRED BY THE TRULY WONDROUS STAGE SHOW, WE LAUNCHED THE WORLD'S FIRST GAY ICE CREAM BAR POP-UP, QUEENS OF THE DESSERT. IN THIS DEN OF DEBAUCHERY IN MAIDEN LANE, COVENT GARDEN, WE INVITED GUESTS TO SADDLE UP FOR SORDID SUNDAES WHILE IN THE WINDOW ICE CREAM POLE DANCER, 'MR WHIPPY', PUT THE 69 INTO A 99, AND VICE CREAM MASSEUR 'JORGE OF THE JUNGLE' OFFERED COMPLEMENTARY ICE CREAM FACIALS AND BODY MASSAGES. WE CREATED A RETRO-COOL CABARET OF CROSS-DRESSING FLAVOURS TO COMPLEMENT THE THEME. CAMPER THAN A ROW OF PINK TENTS FILLED WITH OODLES OF DOUBLE ENTENDRE, THIS WHITE CHOCOLATE ICE CREAM DOESN'T DRAG, IT SINGS.

- 250ml (8fl oz) full-fat milk • 125ml (4fl oz) double cream • 2 egg yolks
- 88g (3¼oz) caster sugar • pinch of sea salt • 100g (3½oz) white chocolate
- 2 heaped tsp Horlicks powder • 2–3 capfuls Irish cream liqueur (such as Baileys)

1. Pour the milk and cream into a large saucepan and heat gently, stirring occasionally, until the mixture begins to steam but not boil.

2. Meanwhile, whisk the egg yolks in a heatproof bowl until smooth. Add the sugar and salt and whisk until pale and slightly fluffy.

3. Gradually and slowly, pour the hot milk into the egg mixture whilst whisking continuously to prevent the eggs scrambling. Return the mixture to the saucepan and place over a low heat, stirring frequently until the custard thinly coats the back of a wooden spoon. Do not allow to boil.

4. Melt the chocolate in a heatproof bowl set over a pan of simmering water. Pour it into the warm custard along with the Horlicks and Irish cream, strring well. Pour the mixture back into the bowl and set aside for about 30 minutes, stirring occasionally, until cooled to room temperature. For more rapid chilling, half-fill a sink with cold water and ice and place the bowl of mixture in it for 20 minutes.

5. Once cooled, cover the mixture and refrigerate, ideally overnight, but at least for 6 hours, until thoroughly chilled (at least 4°C). Pour the chilled mixture into an ice cream machine and churn according to the manufacturer's instructions. If making by hand, see the instructions on page 15.

6. When the churning is completed, use a spoon or spatula to scrape the ice cream into a freezer-proof container with a lid. Freeze until it reaches the correct scooping texture (at least 2 hours).

Inside scoop VIRGINAL WHITE STICKY CHOCOLATE SHOT THROUGH WITH A SUBLIMINAL ZAP OF MALTED HORLICKS, VIOLATED WITH A CHEEKY SPLASH OF IRISH CREAM LIQUEUR

USED IN »

NUCLEAR WINTER

PG 136

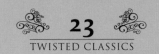
CHOC AND AWE

DARK CHOCOLATE ICE CREAM

MAKE ICE CREAM NOT WAR, WITH THIS INTENSE CHOCOLATE ICE CREAM THAT RUNS LIKE A MIND-MELTING MELODY. RIFFING ON 70% COCOA NOTES, STRONG, EARTHY FRUIT TONES AND A VELVETY MOUTHFEEL, IT WILL SATIATE YOUR DARKEST DESIRES AND TRANSPORT ADDICTS TO CHOCOLATE NIRVANA. EACH TYPE OF CHOCOLATE IMPARTS ITS OWN FLAVOUR STAMP BASED ON ITS PROVENANCE. WE USE VENEZUELAN, ECUADOREAN AND SOMETIMES GHANAIAN CHOCOLATE.

- 250ml (8fl oz) full-fat milk • 125ml (4fl oz) double cream
- 2 egg yolks • 88g (3¼oz) caster sugar • 50g (2oz) cocoa powder
- 150g (5oz) dark chocolate (at least 70% cocoa solids), finely chopped

1. Pour the milk and cream into a large saucepan and heat gently, stirring occasionally, until the mixture begins to steam but not boil.

2. Meanwhile, whisk the egg yolks in a heatproof bowl until smooth. Add the caster sugar and whisk until pale and slightly fluffy.

3. Take the milk off the heat and whisk in the cocoa powder. Add the chocolate and stir until completely melted. Gradually and slowly, pour the chocolate milk into the egg mixture whilst whisking continuously to prevent the eggs scrambling. Return the mixture to the saucepan and place over a low heat, stirring frequently until the custard thinly coats the back of a wooden spoon. Do not allow to boil.

4. Pour the mixture back into the bowl and set aside for about 30 minutes, stirring occasionally, until cooled to room temperature. For more rapid chilling, half-fill a sink with cold water and ice and place the bowl of mixture in it for 20 minutes. Never put the hot mixture into the fridge.

5. Once cooled, cover the mixture and refrigerate, ideally overnight, but at least for 6 hours, until thoroughly chilled (at least 4°C). Pour the chilled mixture into an ice cream machine and churn according to the manufacturer's instructions. If making by hand, see the instructions on page 15.

6. When the churning is completed, use a spoon or spatula to scrape the ice cream into a freezer-proof container with a lid. Freeze until it reaches the correct scooping texture (at least 2 hours).

I SCOOP, THEREFORE I AM

A THUNDERING ASSAULT ON THE SENSES, THIS RICH, CHOCOLATE GANACHE-STYLE
ICE CREAM DELIVERS A THRILLING BLITZKRIEG OF COCOA KICKS

Inside scoop

USED IN ≫

THE FEDERICI

PG 140

SEX, DRUGS AND CHOC 'N' ROLL

MILK CHOCOLATE ICE CREAM

FIGHT FOR YOUR RIGHT TO SELF-MEDICATE WITH THE NATION'S FAVOURITE NARCOTIC. THIS MILD, ELEGANT, CREAMY RECIPE HAS AN EDGY SEA SALT HINT THAT ELEVATES A COMFORTING MILKY MOMENT INTO SOMETHING MORE WONKY THAN WONKA. TO PARAPHRASE THE WORDS OF IAN DURY – HIT ME WITH YOUR LICKING STICK, HIT ME, HIT ME.

- 250ml (8fl oz) full-fat milk • 125ml (4fl oz) double cream • 2 egg yolks
- 88g (3¼oz) caster sugar • pinch sea salt • 25g (1oz) cocoa powder
- 100g (3½oz) milk chocolate, finely chopped, plus extra for sprinkles

1. Pour the milk and cream into a large saucepan and heat gently, stirring occasionally, until the mixture begins to steam but not boil.

2. Meanwhile, whisk the egg yolks in a heatproof bowl until smooth. Add the caster sugar and salt and whisk until pale and slightly fluffy.

3. Take the milk off the heat and whisk in the cocoa powder. Add the chocolate and stir until completely melted. Gradually and slowly, pour the chocolate milk into the egg mixture whilst whisking continuously to prevent the eggs scrambling. Return the mixture to the saucepan and place over a low heat, stirring frequently until the custard thinly coats the back of a wooden spoon. Do not allow to boil.

4. Pour the mixture back into the bowl and set aside for about 30 minutes, stirring occasionally, until cooled to room temperature. For more rapid chilling, half-fill a sink with

cold water and ice and place the bowl of mixture in it for 20 minutes. Never put the hot mixture into the fridge.

5. Once cooled, cover the mixture and refrigerate, ideally overnight, but at least for 6 hours, until thoroughly chilled (at least 4°C). Pour the chilled mixture into an ice cream machine and churn according to the manufacturer's instructions. If making by hand, see the instructions on page 15.

6. When the churning is completed, use a spoon or spatula to scrape the ice cream into a freezer-proof container with a lid. Freeze until it reaches the correct scooping texture (at least 2 hours). Use a cheese slicer or grater to make chocolate sprinkles to decorate.

ANARCHY IN THE UK ... WITH SPRINKLES

A DELIRIOUS CREAM TEASE OF BUTTERY COCOA NOTES

USED IN

THE JUGGERNAUT

PG 128

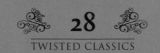
A CHOCWORK ORANGE

DARK CHOCOLATE & ORANGE

THE ICECREAMISTS ARE MORE SID AND NANCY THAN BEN AND JERRY, SO OUR FOCUS GROUPS ARE MORE LIKE SUBVERSIVE INTERROGATIONS. WE BLINDFOLDED 40 OF OUR FANS AND SUBJECTED THEM TO AN EXTREME ICE CREAM TASTING. THE FIRST FLAVOUR WE TRIED WAS THIS BITTER-SWEET ORGY OF DECADENT COCOA AND ORANGE. ON THE BASIS OF THE RESPONSES, WE HAVE ENOUGH EVIDENCE TO PLACE THIS ICE CREAM ON AN ASSAULT CHARGE.

· 250ml (8fl oz) full-fat milk · 125ml (4fl oz) double cream · 2 egg yolks
· 88g (3¼oz) caster sugar · 50g (2oz) cocoa powder
· 150g (5oz) dark chocolate (at least 70% cocoa solids), finely chopped
· 65ml (2½fl oz) orange extract, or to taste · zest of ½ an orange, to decorate

1. Pour the milk and cream into a large saucepan and heat gently, stirring occasionally, until the mixture begins to steam but not boil.

2. Meanwhile, whisk the egg yolks in a heatproof bowl until smooth. Add the caster sugar and whisk until pale and slightly fluffy.

3. Take the milk off the heat and whisk in the cocoa powder. Add the chocolate and orange extract and stir until completely melted. Gradually and slowly, pour the chocolate milk into the egg mixture whilst whisking continuously to prevent the eggs scrambling. Return the mixture to the saucepan and place over a low heat, stirring frequently until the custard thinly coats the back of a wooden spoon. Do not allow to boil.

4. Pour the mixture back into the bowl and set aside for about 30 minutes, stirring occasionally, until cooled to room temperature. For more rapid chilling, half-fill a sink with cold water and ice and place the bowl of mixture in it for 20 minutes. Never put the hot mixture into the fridge.

5. Once cooled, cover the mixture and refrigerate, ideally overnight, but at least for 6 hours, until thoroughly chilled (at least 4°C). Pour the chilled mixture into an ice cream machine and churn according to the manufacturer's instructions. If making by hand, see the instructions on page 15.

6. When the churning is completed, use a spoon or spatula to scrape the ice cream into a freezer-proof container with a lid. Freeze until it reaches the correct scooping texture (at least 2 hours).

7. Decorate each portion with orange zest before serving.

A CHILLING MIX OF COCOA KICKS AND ORANGE LICKS

USED IN ⟩⟩ FIRE & VICE
PG 114

GINGIANA JONES
ASIAN SPICED GINGER ICE CREAM

A WHIP-CRACKING MIX OF GROUND GINGER, SYRUP-RICH STEM GINGER AND CRYSTALLIZED GINGER THAT COMBINES EASTERN HEAT WITH COOLING CREAM. DON'T BE DECEIVED BY ITS MATURE APPEARANCE, THIS ICE CREAM WILL STALK YOU, THEN GRIP YOU BY YOUR THROAT LIKE THE INSIDIOUS FU MANCHU, BEFORE THROWING YOU ON THE FLOOR AND DELIVERING A VISCERAL SMACK OF HEAT TO YOUR CHOPS. HEE-YA!

- 250ml (8fl oz) full-fat milk · 125ml (4fl oz) double cream · 2 egg yolks
- 88g (3¼oz) caster sugar · 1½ heaped tbsp ground ginger
- 3 balls of stem ginger · 1 tbsp stem ginger syrup
- 50g (2oz) crystallized ginger, finely chopped, plus extra to decorate

1. Pour the milk and cream into a large saucepan and heat gently, stirring occasionally, until the mixture begins to steam but not boil.

2. Meanwhile, whisk the egg yolks in a heatproof bowl until smooth. Add the sugar and whisk until pale and slightly fluffy. Gradually and slowly, pour the hot milk into the egg mixture whilst whisking continuously to prevent the eggs scrambling. Return the mixture to the saucepan and place over a low heat, stirring frequently until the custard thinly coats the back of a wooden spoon. Do not allow to boil.

3. Add the ground ginger, stem ginger and syrup and mix using a stick blender. Pour the mixture back into the bowl and set aside for about 30 minutes, stirring occasionally, until cooled to room temperature. For more rapid chilling, half-fill a sink with cold water and ice and place the bowl of mixture in it for 20 minutes. Never put the hot mixture into the fridge.

4. Once cooled, cover the mixture and refrigerate, ideally overnight, but at least for 6 hours, until thoroughly chilled (at least 4°C). Pour the chilled mixture into an ice cream machine and churn according to the manufacturer's instructions. If making by hand, see the instructions on page 15.

5. When the churning is completed, fold the crystallized ginger into the ice cream, then use a spoon or spatula to scrape the mixture into a freezer-proof container with a lid. Freeze until it reaches the correct scooping texture (at least 2 hours).

6. Decorate each serving with some finely chopped crystallized ginger.

GET YOUR KICKS WITH OUR LICKS

SET LIGHT TO THE FUSE AND WATCH IT BURN. BEAUTIFULLY OFFSET BY THE SUGARY AMALGAM OF CYSTALLIZED GINGER.

Inside scoop

TAKING THE PISTACCHIO
PISTACCHIO ICE CREAM

WHILE YOU CAN SOURCE GREAT PISTACCHIOS FROM IRAN AND ITALY, THE BEST IN THE WORLD ARE THE 'GREEN GOLD' OF SICILY, FROM THE PISTACCHIO CAPITAL OF BRONTE. GROWN ON THE LAVA SOIL OF MOUNT ETNA, THESE SMOKY, OCHRE-GREEN JEWELS CARRY A SWEET, DELICATE AROMA THAT CAN RENDER THE MOST OUTSPOKEN AFICIONADO SPEECHLESS IN A MAFIOSO-STYLE CODE OF SILENCE. SICILIANS CURIOUSLY ALLEGE THAT THE PISTACCHIO CAN 'EXCITE THE ARDOURS OF VENUS AND INCREASE THE FEMININE HUMOUR'. FOR US IT'S THE ULTIMATE NUT JOB. FOR A TOTALLY NUTTY TWIST YOU CAN REPLACE THE PISTACCHIOS WITH HAZELNUTS.

· 250ml (8fl oz) full-fat milk · 125ml (4fl oz) double cream · 2 egg yolks
· 88g (3¼oz) caster sugar · pinch of sea salt
· 125g (4oz) shelled unsalted pistacchio nuts, plus a few extra to decorate
· dash of almond extract (about ¼ teaspoon)

1. Preheat your oven to 150°C/Gas 1. Spread 100g (3½oz) of the pistacchios on a baking tray and place in the oven for 10 minutes, until lightly browned. This will release locked-in flavour. Allow to cool a little, then put into a coffee grinder or food processor and grind to a fine powder. Transfer to a small bowl, add the almond extract and mix well.

2. Pour the milk and cream into a large saucepan and heat gently, stirring occasionally, until the mixture begins to steam but not boil. Meanwhile, whisk the egg yolks in a heatproof bowl until smooth. Add the sugar and salt and whisk until pale and slightly fluffy. Gradually and slowly, pour the hot milk into the egg mixture whilst whisking continuously to prevent the eggs scrambling.

3. Return the mixture to the saucepan and place over a low heat. Add the pistacchio powder and cook, stirring frequently, until the custard thinly coats the back of a wooden spoon. Do not allow to boil. Whilst hot, whizz the mixture thoroughly with a stick blender. Strain into a bowl – once through a fine sieve, and then through a muslin cloth to remove all the nut pieces but leave the flavour, then stir in the almond extract.

4. Set aside for about 30 minutes, stirring occasionally, until cooled to room temperature. For more rapid chilling, half-fill a sink with cold water and ice and place the bowl of mixture in it for 20 minutes. Never put the hot mixture into the fridge.

5. Once cooled, cover the mixture and refrigerate, ideally overnight, but at least for 6 hours, until thoroughly chilled (at least 4°C). Pour the chilled mixture into an ice cream machine and churn according to the manufacturer's instructions. If making by hand, see the instructions on page 15.

6. When the churning is completed, chop the remaining pistacchios and fold into the ice cream. Use a spoon or spatula to scrape the ice cream into a freezer-proof container with a lid and freeze until it reaches the correct scooping texture (at least 2 hours).

7. Decorate each serving with chopped pistacchios.

A POETICALLY BALANCED ICE CREAM WITH WONDERFUL NUTTY NOTES THAT WILL
LEAVE YOU REACHING FOR YOUR THESAURUS

Inside scoop

USED IN »

THE OMERTA

PG 111

NUTS ABOUT CHOCLAND YARD
HAZELNUT CHOCOLATE ICE CREAM

I WAS BANNED FROM ENTERING LONDON DURING THE STATE OPENING OF PARLIAMENT IN 2005, ON THE GROUNDS THAT THE METROPOLITAN POLICE COULD NOT 'GUARANTEE' MY SAFETY SO I STAYED AT HOME AND MADE THIS ICE CREAM INSTEAD. DESCRIBED BY MY ARRESTING OFFICERS AS A CURFEW-BREAKING BLEND OF CREAM AND HAZELNUT CHOCOLATE THAT WOULD BE USED IN EVIDENCE AGAINST ME DO I LOVE THIS ICE CREAM? GUILTY AS CHARGED, YOUR HONOUR.

· 250ml (8fl oz) full-fat milk · 125ml (4fl oz) double cream · 2 egg yolks
· 88g (3¼oz) caster sugar · 150g (5oz) hazelnut chocolate spread (such as Nutella)

1. Pour the milk and cream into a large saucepan and heat gently, stirring occasionally, until the mixture begins to steam but not boil.

2. Meanwhile, whisk the egg yolks in a heatproof bowl until smooth. Add the caster sugar and whisk until pale and slightly fluffy.

3. Take the milk off the heat and whisk in the hazelnut chocolate spread until blended. Gradually and slowly, pour the chocolate milk into the egg mixture whilst whisking continuously to prevent the eggs scrambling. Return the mixture to the saucepan and place over a low heat, stirring frequently until the custard thinly coats the back of a wooden spoon. Do not allow to boil.

4. Pour the mixture back into the bowl and set aside for about 30 minutes, stirring occasionally, until cooled to room temperature. For more rapid chilling, half-fill a sink with cold water and ice and place the bowl of mixture in it for 20 minutes. Never put the hot mixture into the fridge.

5. Once cooled, cover the mixture and refrigerate, ideally overnight, but at least for 6 hours, until thoroughly chilled (at least 4°C). Pour the chilled mixture into an ice cream machine and churn according to the manufacturer's instructions. If making by hand, see the instructions on page 15.

6. When the churning is completed, use a spoon or spatula to scrape the ice cream into a freezer-proof container with a lid. Freeze until it reaches the correct scooping texture (at least 2 hours).

7. To create a great chocolate sauce, place 6 tablespoons of Nutella in a heatproof bowl or jug and microwave for 60 seconds on medium, stirring every 20 seconds, then pour over your ice cream. Bellissimo!

PUT YOUR CLOTHES ON AND I'LL BUY YOU AN ICE CREAM JAMES BOND

Inside scoop THE BASIS FOR NUTELLA IS GIANDUIA, A CHOCOLATE AND HAZELNUT CONCOCTION CREATED IN TURIN, WHICH BECAME POPULAR DURING WORLD WAR II WHEN COCOA WAS IN SHORT SUPPLY AND HAZELNUT PASTE WAS USED AS A SUBSTITUTE.

CARAMELTDOWN
DULCE DE LECHE ICE CREAM

YOU'RE IN THE MIDDLE OF A 21ST-CENTURY MELTDOWN: YOUR BANK IS BUST AND THE CASHPOINTS ARE EMPTY. FEAR NOT, BECAUSE IN A TIME OF ADVERSITY LIES OPPORTUNITY. IN THIS CASE, THE CARAMELTDOWN – A WARM, SILKY CUSTARD BASE WITH DULCE DE LECHE, AN ARGENTINE BUTTERSCOTCH-'CONDENSED-MILK'-TOFFEE-CHEW KICK. THIS SEDUCTIVE ORAL LUBRICANT WILL LEAVE YOU DEFROSTING HELPLESSLY IN A PUDDLE ON THE FLOOR AS THE WORLD COLLAPSES AROUND YOU. DON'T CRY FOR ME ARGENTINA? IT'LL BE THE REST OF THE WORLD THAT'S REACHING FOR THE TISSUES AFTER YOU'VE LICKED THIS NUMBER.

• 250ml (8fl oz) full-fat milk • 125ml (4fl oz) double cream • 2 egg yolks
• 88g (3¼oz) caster sugar • large pinch of sea salt
• 250ml (8fl oz) Dulce de Leche sauce (see page 154), plus a little extra for drizzling

1. Pour the milk and cream into a large saucepan and heat gently, stirring occasionally, until the mixture begins to steam but not boil.

2. Meanwhile, whisk the egg yolks in a heatproof bowl until smooth. Add the sugar and salt and whisk until pale and slightly fluffy. Gradually and slowly, pour the hot milk into the egg mixture whilst whisking continuously to prevent the eggs scrambling. Return the mixture to the saucepan and place over a low heat, stirring frequently until the custard thinly coats the back of a wooden spoon. Do not allow to boil.

3. Pour back into the bowl and set aside for about 30 minutes, stirring occasionally, until cooled to room temperature. For more rapid chilling, half-fill a sink with cold water and ice and place the bowl of mixture in it for 20 minutes. Never put the hot mixture into the fridge.

4. Once cooled, cover the mixture and refrigerate, ideally overnight, but at least for 6 hours, until thoroughly chilled (at least 4°C).

5. Add 100ml (3½fl oz) of the Dulce de Leche sauce to the chilled mixture and combine well with a stick blender. Pour into an ice cream machine and churn according to the manufacturer's instructions. If making by hand, see the instructions on page 15.

6. Just before the churning is finished, warm another 100ml (3½fl oz) of the sauce in a heatproof bowl or jug and microwave on medium for 20–30 seconds to loosen. Gradually pour the sauce into the ice cream for the last 2 minutes of churning. When the churning is completed, use a spoon or spatula to scrape the ice cream into a freezer-proof container with a lid. Freeze until it reaches the correct scooping texture (at least 2 hours).

7. Drizzle each serving with the remaining sauce, gently warmed.

CAPITALISM SUCKS

Inside scoop

DULCE DE LECHE MEANS 'SWEET MILK' AND IT IS PREPARED BY SLOWLY HEATING SWEETENED MILK TO CREATE A CARAMELIZED SUGAR FLAVOUR THAT IS FIENDISHLY SEDUCTIVE

USED IN ⟩⟩ MOLOTOFFEE

PG 120

THE CUSTARDY SUITE
TRADITIONAL ITALIAN CREMA ICE CREAM

DURING MY TIME AT THE UNIVERSITY OF ADVERSITY, I'VE BEEN BOILED, SCRAMBLED, POACHED AND FRIED IN MANY A CUSTODY SUITE BY OVER-ENTHUSIASTIC LAW ENFORCMENT OFFICERS. THIS ICE CREAM, A TRADITIONAL ITALIAN CREMA, IS ANOTHER ARRESTING EXPERIENCE THAT WILL LEAVE DEFENDANTS DIALLING 999 TO CONFESS TO A REPEAT OFFENCE. IT IS AN EGGIER VARIATION OF OUR BASE MIX, AND ALL THE MORE DELICIOUS FOR IT. UNADULTERATED EGGSTACY!

· 250ml (8fl oz) full-fat milk · 125ml (4fl oz) double cream · 4 egg yolks · 88g (3¼oz) caster sugar · pinch of sea salt

1. Pour the milk and cream into a large saucepan and heat gently, stirring occasionally, until the mixture begins to steam but not boil.

2. Meanwhile, whisk the egg yolks in a heatproof bowl until smooth. Add the sugar and salt and whisk until pale and slightly fluffy. Gradually and slowly, pour the hot milk into the egg mixture whilst whisking continuously to prevent the eggs scrambling. Return the mixture to the saucepan and place over a low heat, stirring frequently until the custard thinly coats the back of a wooden spoon. Do not allow to boil.

3. Pour back into the bowl and set aside for about 30 minutes, stirring occasionally, until cooled to room temperature. For more rapid chilling, half-fill a sink with cold water and ice and place the bowl of mixture in it for 20 minutes. Never put the hot mixture into the fridge.

4. Once cooled, cover the mixture and refrigerate, ideally overnight, but at least for 6 hours, until thoroughly chilled (at least 4°C). Pour the chilled mixture into an ice cream machine and churn according to the manufacturer's instructions. If making by hand, see the instructions on page 15.

5. When the churning is completed, use a spoon or spatula to scrape the ice cream into a freezer-proof container with a lid. Freeze until it reaches the correct scooping texture (at least 2 hours).

GOD SAVE THE CREAM

AN INTENSELY RICH, CUSTARDY FLAVOUR WITH A THICK, LUSTROUS MOUTHFEEL

Inside scoop

USED IN ≫ MANTECATO ITALIANO
PG 138

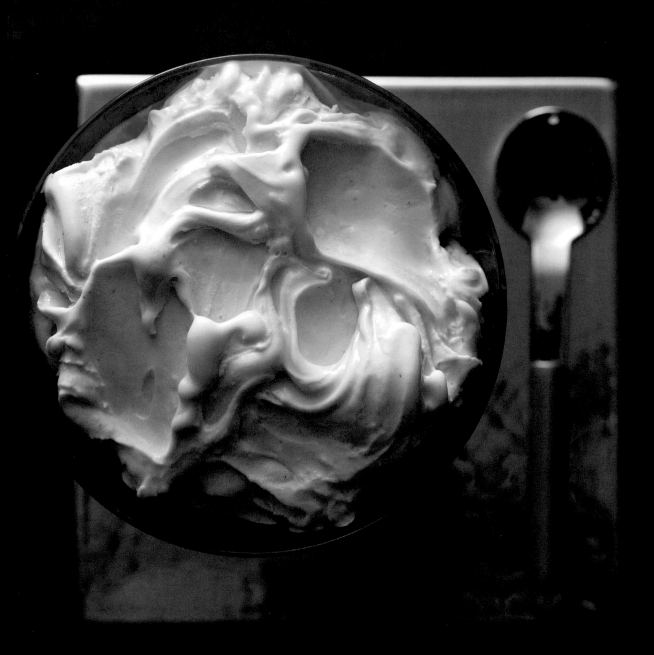

DESSERT STORM
TIRAMISU ICE CREAM

MY WIFE NADINE AND I ARRIVED FOR OUR NUPTIALS IN AN ICE CREAM VAN EMBLAZONED WITH THE BANNER 'WEDLOCKED: THERE ARE SOME INSTITUTIONS YOU CAN'T ESCAPE FROM'. THE NIGHT OF THE WEDDING, MY BROTHER DAVID AND I DISCUSSED THE MERITS OF A TIRAMISU ICE CREAM AND DECIDED IT WAS THE ULTIMATE DESSERT STORM, BUT WHAT WAS THE PERFECT COMBO OF INGREDIENTS? MORE MARSALA WINE? SAVOIARDI SPONGE FINGERS? AS THE DEBATE RAGED INTO THE NIGHT, I TOLD MY INCREASINGLY IMPATIENT WIFE, 'I'LL BE AT THE MARITAL SUITE BY 11.30 P.M. IF I'M LATE, START WITHOUT ME.'

- 250ml (8fl oz) full-fat milk · 125ml (4fl oz) double cream · 2 egg yolks
- 88g (3¼oz) muscovado sugar · pinch of sea salt · 4 sponge finger biscuits,
preferably Savoiardi · 88g (3¼oz) mascarpone cheese · 150ml (5fl oz) Marsala wine
- 1 capful Kahlua liqueur · 1 capful dark rum · cocoa powder, to dust

FOR THE SYRUP · 100g (3½oz) caster sugar · 3 heaped tsp instant coffee granules

1. Pour the milk and cream into a large saucepan and heat gently, stirring occasionally, until the mixture begins to steam but not boil.

2. Meanwhile, whisk the egg yolks in a heatproof bowl until smooth. Add the sugar and salt and whisk until slightly fluffy. Gradually and slowly, pour the hot milk into the egg mixture whilst whisking continuously to prevent the eggs scrambling. Return the mixture to the saucepan and place over a low heat, stirring frequently until the custard thinly coats the back of a wooden spoon. Do not allow to boil.

3. Pour back into the bowl and set aside for about 30 minutes, stirring occasionally, until cooled to room temperature. For more rapid chilling, half-fill a sink with cold water and ice and place the bowl of mixture in it for 20 minutes. Never put the hot mixture into the fridge. Once cooled, cover the mixture and refrigerate, ideally overnight, but at least for 6 hours, until thoroughly chilled (at least 4°C).

4. Meanwhile, make the syrup. Put the caster sugar and 100ml (3½fl oz) water into a pan and whisk over a low heat until the sugar dissolves. Add the coffee granules and simmer while whisking, until the liquid turns into a syrup.

5. Put the sponge fingers on a plate and drizzle the syrup over them. Set aside.

6. Using a spoon, fold the mascarpone into the cold custard, then stir in the Marsala. Pour the mixture into an ice cream machine, add the Kahlua and rum and churn according to manufacturer's instructions. If making by hand, see the instructions on page 15.

7. When the churning is completed, use a spoon or spatula to scrape the ice cream into a freezer-proof container, topping the ice cream with one layer of syrupy sponge fingers. Dust with cocoa powder, place the lid on and freeze until it reaches the correct scooping texture (at least 2 hours).

8. Lightly dust each portion with cocoa powder before serving.

TIRAMISU IS ITALIAN FOR 'PICK ME UP'. THIS SUB-ZERO INTERPRETATION ISN'T ANY OLD PICK-ME-UP – IT'S AN INTERNATIONAL ABDUCTION!

Inside scoop

LIVING IN CINNAMON
APPLE AND CINNAMON ICE CREAM

AS OSCAR WILDE ONCE SAID, 'I CAN RESIST EVERYTHING EXCEPT TEMPTATION.' IN THIS CASE, A FRENCH TOPLESS MODEL AND CONSEQUENT 'DEPLORABLE ATTENDANCE RECORD' RESULTING IN MY EXPULSION FROM ART COLLEGE. SUCH WERE THE EDUCATIONAL DISTRACTIONS OF LIVING IN SIN. HER FATHER PATRICK, WHO LIVED IN PARIS AND RAN A MAGAZINE FOR THE ASSOCIATION OF BARMEN IN FRANCE, INITIATED ME INTO THE ART OF DECADENCE, CULTIVATING MY TASTE FOR MONTECRISTO CIGARS, FINE ARMAGNAC AND SEDUCTIVE SPICES LIKE CINNAMON...

- 250ml (8fl oz) full-fat milk · 125ml (4fl oz) double cream · 2 egg yolks
- 88g (3¼oz) caster sugar · 100g (3½oz) apple sauce
- 2 tsp ground cinnamon , plus extra for dusting
- 100ml (3½fl oz) balsamic vinegar (optional)

1. Pour the milk and cream into a large saucepan and heat gently, stirring occasionally, until the mixture begins to steam but not boil.

2. Meanwhile, whisk the egg yolks in a heatproof bowl until smooth. Add the sugar and whisk until pale and slightly fluffy. Gradually and slowly, pour the hot milk into the egg mixture whilst whisking continuously to prevent the eggs scrambling. Return the mixture to the saucepan and place over a low heat, stirring frequently until the custard thinly coats the back of a wooden spoon. Do not allow to boil.

3. Pour back into the bowl and set aside for about 30 minutes, stirring occasionally, until cooled to room temperature. For more rapid chilling, half-fill a sink with cold water and ice and place the bowl of mixture in it for 20 minutes. Never put the hot mixture into the fridge.

4. Once cooled, cover the mixture and refrigerate, ideally overnight, but at least for 6 hours, until thoroughly chilled (at least 4°C).

5. Add the apple sauce and cinnamon to the chilled mixture and combine well with a stick blender. Pour into an ice cream machine and churn according to the manufacturer's instructions. If making by hand, see the instructions on page 15.

6. When the churning is completed, gradually fold in the balsamic (if using). Use a spoon or spatula to scrape the ice cream into a freezer-proof container with a lid, then freeze until it reaches the correct scooping texture (at least 2 hours).

7. Dust each portion with extra cinnamon before serving.

GIVE IT A SWIRL

THIS IS A POETIC COMBINATION OF TART APPLE, OFFSET BY A BITTER-SWEET SMIDGEN OF NORTH AFRICAN CINNAMON AND A DASH OF SUGAR

Inside scoop

SCARLETT FEVER
STRAWBERRY AND BALSAMIC ICE CREAM

BLESSED ARE THE LIPS OF THE ACTRESS SCARLETT JOHANSSON – A ONE-WOMAN WARM FRONT WITH A SMOULDERING, FULL-BODIED POUT THAT COULD MAKE A LOLLIPOP TOO HAPPY. NOW, YOU MAY BE THINKING HOW DOES SCARLETT RELATE TO STRAWBERRIES? FOR SOME PERVERSE PSYCHOLOGICAL REASONING KNOWN ONLY TO MY PSYCHIATRIST, A GREAT-LOOKING STRAWBERRY REMINDED ME OF THE FRUITIEST SMACKERS IN THE WORLD. WE DEDICATE THIS ICE CREAM TO HER, SO PUCKER UP FOR A DOSE OF SCARLETT FEVER.

• 250ml (8fl oz) full-fat milk • 125ml (4fl oz) double cream • 2 egg yolks
• 60g (2¼oz) caster sugar •

FOR THE STRAWBERRY SYRUP • 200g (7oz) strawberries, hulled and chopped • 60g (2¼oz) caster sugar • juice of ½ a lemon FOR THE BALSAMIC REDUCTION • 100ml (3½fl oz) balsamic vinegar • caster sugar, to taste

1. First make the syrup. Put all the syrup ingredients into a saucepan and place over a low heat until simmering gently and the strawberries are softening. Simmer for about 5 minutes, stirring occasionally, then pour into a heatproof bowl.

2. Half-fill a sink with cold water and ice and place the bowl of syrup in it for 20 minutes. Never put the hot mixture into the fridge. Once cooled, cover the syrup and refrigerate, ideally overnight, but at least for 6 hours, until thoroughly chilled (at least 4°C).

3. Pour the milk and cream into a large saucepan and heat gently, stirring occasionally, until it begins to steam but not boil.

4. Meanwhile, whisk the egg yolks in a heatproof bowl until smooth. Add the sugar and whisk until pale and slightly fluffy. Gradually and slowly, pour the hot milk into the egg mixture whilst whisking continuously to prevent the eggs scrambling. Return the mixture to the saucepan and place over a low heat, stirring frequently until the custard thinly coats the back of a wooden spoon. Do not allow to boil.

5. Pour back into the bowl and set aside for about 30 minutes, stirring occasionally, until cooled to room temperature. For more rapid chilling, half-fill a sink with cold water and ice and place the bowl of mixture in it for 20 minutes. Never put the hot mixture into the fridge. Once cooled, cover and refrigerate, ideally overnight, but at least for 6 hours, until thoroughly chilled (at least 4°C).

6. Using a spoon, stir three-quarters of the syrup into the chilled mixture: do not use a blender as you want to keep the texture of the strawberry pieces. Pour into an ice cream machine and churn according to the manufacturer's instructions, adding the remainder of the strawberry syrup about 5 minutes before the end. If making by hand, see the instructions on page 15.

7. When the churning is completed, use a spoon or spatula to scrape the ice cream into a freezer-proof container with a lid. Freeze until it reaches scooping texture (at least 2 hours).

8. Meanwhile, put the balsamic vinegar into a pan on a moderate heat and whisk briskly until it reduces by about half and becomes syrupy. Add a little caster sugar to taste if required.

9. Offer the reduction with the ice cream: the seemingly implausible combo of balsamic and strawberry works very successfully.

WE MEAN EVERY SYLLABLE WHEN WE SAY THIS IS A SEDUCTIVE COMBO OF FRESH CREAM CUT THROUGH WITH ZINGY STRAWBERRY FLAVOUR. DEFINITELY NOT JUST LIP SERVICE...

Inside scoop

USED IN ⟩⟩

STRAWBERRY ICEQUAKE

PG 126

MINT CONDITION
MINT CHOCOLATE ICE CREAM

ONCE UPON A TIME ON ST GEORGE'S DAY, SCOTTISH POLICE WERE FORCED TO SURROUND BEN NEVIS AFTER RUMOURS CIRCULATED THAT I PLANNED TO MARK THE DAY BY PLANTING THE CROSS OF ST GEORGE ON THE PEAK WHILST DRESSED IN A SUIT OF ARMOUR. AS ANY FOOL COULD HAVE TOLD YOU, I WASN'T IN MINT CONDITION. I WOULD HAVE STRUGGLED TO SCALE A TOILET IN THAT GET-UP, LET ALONE CLIMB A MOUNTAIN. ONE OF THE BEST THINGS I DISCOVERED ABOUT SCOTLAND IN MY TRAVAILS WAS THEIR LOVE OF MINTS. I CAME ACROSS THIS ICE CREAM IDEA IN A SMALL PARLOUR ON THE WEST COAST OF SCOTLAND – MASHED-UP AFTER EIGHT MINTS IN A DELICIOUS GOOEY, SUGARY RIPPLE, CUT THROUGH WITH FRESH MINT AND BITTER CHOCOLATE.

• 250ml (8fl oz) full-fat milk • 125ml (4fl oz) double cream • 2 egg yolks • 88g (3¼oz) caster sugar • 120g (3¾oz) dark chocolate fondant mints, such as After Eight mints, roughly chopped

1. Pour the milk and cream into a large saucepan and heat gently, stirring occasionally, until the mixture begins to steam but not boil.

2. Meanwhile, whisk the egg yolks in a heatproof bowl until smooth. Add the sugar and whisk until pale and slightly fluffy. Gradually and slowly, pour the hot milk into the egg mixture whilst whisking continuously to prevent the eggs scrambling. Return the mixture to the saucepan and place over a low heat, stirring frequently until the custard thinly coats the back of a wooden spoon. Do not allow to boil.

3. Pour the mixture back into the bowl and set aside for about 30 minutes, stirring occasionally, until cooled to room temperature. For more rapid chilling, half-fill a sink with cold water and ice and place the bowl of mixture in it for 20 minutes. Never put the hot mixture into the fridge. Meanwhile melt the fondant mints in a heatproof bowl over a pan of simmering water.

4. Once the ice cream mixture is cooled, add the melted chocolate mints to the bowl, along with the mixture, blend with a stick blender and refrigerate, ideally overnight, but at least for 6 hours, until thoroughly chilled (at least 4°C). Pour the chilled mixture into an ice cream machine and churn according to the manufacturer's instructions. If making by hand, see page 15.

5. When the churning is completed, fold in the After Eight mints with a spoon or spatula, and scrape the ice cream into a freezer-proof container with a lid. Freeze until it reaches the correct scooping texture (at least 2 hours).

6. Decorate each portion with fresh mint leaves before serving.

THE ICE CREAM MAN COMETH

A DEVASTATING MASH-UP OF FRESH MINT, CREAM AND DARK CHOCOLATE FONDANT MINTS

Inside scoop

UNDER THE CHERRY SPOON

MASCARPONE AND AMARENA CHERRY ICE CREAM

NICOLA FABBRI IS THE FASHIONABLY ELEGANT PROPRIETOR OF FABBRI, PURVEYORS OF THE FINEST AMARENA CHERRIES IN THE WORLD, WHICH ARE SOLD IN ICONIC WHITE AND BLUE CERAMIC JARS. THIS ICE CREAM IS INSPIRED BY MY VISIT TO THEIR FACTORY IN BOLOGNA IN THE BLISTERING SUMMER HEAT OF 2009. NICOLA'S ENGLISH WAS NEVER VERY GOOD, BUT WHEN IT CAME TO BEATING THE MASS-MARKET COMPETITION, HE WAS EXTRAORDINARILY FLUENT 'YES, WHEN YOU F*&K THEM, YOU TELL ME HOW HARD YOU F*&K THEM.'

- 250ml (8fl oz) full-fat milk • 125ml (4fl oz) double cream • 2 egg yolks
- 88g (3¼oz) caster sugar • pinch of sea salt • 250g (8oz) mascarpone cheese
- 200g (7oz) Amarena cherries, plus a few extra to decorate

1. Pour the milk and cream into a large saucepan and heat gently, stirring occasionally, until the mixture begins to steam but not boil.

2. Meanwhile, whisk the egg yolks in a heatproof bowl until smooth. Add the sugar and salt and whisk until pale and slightly fluffy. Gradually and slowly, pour the hot milk into the egg mixture whilst whisking continuously to prevent the eggs scrambling. Return the mixture to the saucepan and place over a low heat, stirring frequently until the custard thinly coats the back of a wooden spoon. Do not allow to boil.

3. Pour back into the bowl and set aside for about 30 minutes, stirring occasionally, until cooled to room temperature. For more rapid chilling, half-fill a sink with cold water and ice and place the bowl of mixture in it for 20 minutes. Never put the hot mixture into the fridge.

4. Once cooled, cover the mixture and refrigerate, ideally overnight, but at least for 6 hours, until thoroughly chilled (at least 4°C).

5. Add the mascarpone to the chilled mixture and combine well with a stick blender. Pour the mixture into an ice cream machine and churn according to the manufacturer's instructions. If making by hand, see the instructions on page 15.

6. When the churning is completed, fold in the cherries, then use a spoon or spatula to scrape the ice cream into a freezer-proof container with a lid. Freeze until it reaches the correct scooping texture (at least 2 hours).

7. Decorate each portion with a few extra cherries before serving.

THE SPOON IS MIGHTIER THAN THE KNIFE – CHANGE YOUR CUTLERY

A SWEET, INTENSE, CLOTTED CREAM-TYPE FLAVOUR, OFFSET BY THE BITE OF THE SLIGHTLY SOUR AMARENA CHERRIES IN SYRUP

Inside scoop

JESUS CHRIST SCOOPERSTAR

FIOR DI LATTE ICE CREAM

ATTEMPTING TO CREATE A REALLY GREAT ICE CREAM IS OFTEN LIKE TRYING TO HANDCUFF LIGHTNING. THE PURITY OF A REALLY GREAT FIOR DI LATTE (FLOWER OF MILK) DEMONSTRATES THIS MORE THAN ANY OTHER ICE CREAM, WITH A FLAVOUR THAT SHOWCASES JUST MILK, CREAM, SUGAR AND A PINCH OF SEA SALT. BECAUSE OF THIS, IT BENEFITS FROM USING THE FINEST INGREDIENTS YOU CAN GET SO THAT THE FLAVOURS SHINE THROUGH. WE INCLUDE IT HERE BECAUSE IT REPRESENTS THE PUREST OF TASTES AND IS ANYTHING BUT VANILLA. IT'S OUR SUPERSTAR FOR SCOOPERSTARS.

- 250ml (8fl oz) full-fat milk • 125ml (4fl oz) double cream • 2 egg yolks
- 88g (3¼oz) caster sugar • pinch of sea salt
- zest of ½ an orange or lemon, to decorate (optional)

1. Pour the milk and cream into a large saucepan and heat gently, stirring occasionally, until the mixture begins to steam but not boil.

2. Meanwhile, whisk the egg yolks in a heatproof bowl until smooth. Add the sugar and salt and whisk until pale and slightly fluffy. Gradually and slowly, pour the hot milk into the egg mixture whilst whisking continuously to prevent the eggs scrambling. Return the mixture to the saucepan and place over a low heat, stirring frequently until the custard thinly coats the back of a wooden spoon. Do not allow to boil.

3. Pour back into the bowl and set aside for about 30 minutes, stirring occasionally, until cooled to room temperature. For more rapid chilling, half-fill a sink with cold water and ice and place the bowl of mixture in it for 20 minutes. Never put the hot mixture into the fridge.

4. Once cooled, cover the mixture and refrigerate, ideally overnight, but at least for 6 hours, until thoroughly chilled (at least 4°C). Pour the chilled mixture into an ice cream machine and churn according to the manufacturer's instructions. If making by hand, see the instructions on page 15.

5. When the churning is completed, use a spoon or spatula to scrape the ice cream into a freezer-proof container with a lid. Freeze until it reaches the correct scooping texture (at least 2 hours).

6. Top each serving with a little orange or lemon zest for a summer twist.

WITH A THICK, CHEWY MOUTHFEEL, THIS IS A CLOSE RELATIVE TO CLOTTED CREAM

Inside scoop

ESPRESSO YOURSELF

COFFEE ICE CREAM

BRING ON THE HYPERTENSION WITH THIS EYE-POPPING, VEIN-THROBBING, JAW-DROPPING, CAFFEINE-FUELLED KICK OF WEAPONS-GRADE ESPRESSO THAT WILL LEAVE YOUR GUESTS DEFIANTLY BOUNCING UP AND DOWN TOPLESS ON MINI-TRAMPOLINES OUTSIDE. IF YOU FANCY, WHY NOT STAGE YOUR OWN BUNGA-BUNGA PARTY IN A CONE WITH TWO SCOOPS, 'BERLUS-CONY'-STYLE?

- 250ml (8fl oz) full-fat milk • 125ml (4fl oz) double cream
- 3 to 4 heaped tsp good-quality instant coffee granules, to taste • 2 egg yolks
- 88g (3¼oz) muscovado sugar • 1 capful Kahlua liqueur, plus extra for drizzling (optional)

1. Pour the milk and cream into a large saucepan, add the coffee granules and heat gently, stirring occasionally, until the mixture begins to steam but not boil.

2. Meanwhile, whisk the egg yolks in a heatproof bowl until smooth. Add the sugar and whisk until slightly fluffy. Gradually and slowly, pour the hot milk into the egg mixture whilst whisking continuously to prevent the eggs scrambling. Return the mixture to the saucepan and place over a low heat, stirring frequently until the custard thinly coats the back of a wooden spoon. Do not allow to boil.

3. Pour back into the bowl and set aside for about 30 minutes, stirring occasionally, until cooled to room temperature. For more rapid chilling, half-fill a sink with cold water and ice and place the bowl of mixture in it for 20 minutes. Never put the hot mixture into the fridge.

4. Once cooled, cover the mixture and refrigerate, ideally overnight, but at least for 6 hours, until thoroughly chilled (at least 4°C).

5. Add the Kahlua (if using), then pour the mixture into an ice cream machine and churn according to the manufacturer's instructions. If making by hand, see the instructions on page 15.

6. When the churning is completed, use a spoon or spatula to scrape the ice cream into a freezer-proof container with a lid. Freeze until it reaches the correct scooping texture (at least 2 hours).

7. Drizzle Kahlua over each serving if you like, or place a scoop of the ice cream in a hot coffee for a decadent affogato.

Inside scoop

A ROBUST BLEND OF COFFEE AND CREAM WITH A SLIGHTLY BURNT FINISH AND TOBACCO NOTES. WE NORMALLY MAKE THIS WITH ESPRESSO, BUT HAVE SIMPLIFIED THE RECIPE SO IT ISN'T NECESSARY.

USED IN

THE GODFATHER
PG 117

THE KISS

LAVENDER ICE CREAM

ATTENTION ALL YOU LADIES IN LAVENDER. AS ROXANNE SAID TO CHRISTIAN, 'YOU GIVE ME MILK INSTEAD OF CREAM.' THERE IS A LESSON HERE THAT SURELY A MAN OF INCOMPARABLE PANACHE, SUCH AS CYRANO DE BERGERAC, WOULD AGREE WITH: NEVER SHORT-CHANGE A LADY ON INGREDIENTS. THIS ICE CREAM IS THE SOFTEST OF KISSES, ELOQUENTLY AND VIVIDLY BROUGHT TO LIFE BY THE LEGEND HIMSELF...

- 250ml (8fl oz) full-fat milk · 125ml (4fl oz) double cream
- 2 egg yolks · 88g (3¼oz) caster sugar ·
- 4 lavender flower heads or a few drops of food-grade lavender oil
- lavender flowers, for decoration · 1 tbsp lavender honey (optional)

1. Pour the milk and cream into a large saucepan and heat gently, stirring occasionally, until the mixture begins to steam but not boil.

2. Meanwhile, whisk the egg yolks in a heatproof bowl until smooth. Add the sugar and whisk until pale and slightly fluffy. Gradually and slowly, pour the hot milk into the egg mixture whilst whisking continuously to prevent the eggs scrambling.

3. Return the mixture to the saucepan and place over a low heat. Add the lavender flower heads or oil and cook, stirring frequently, until the custard thinly coats the back of a wooden spoon. Do not allow to boil. If using lavender flower heads, use a stick blender to pulse the custard and release the flavour.

4. Pour the mixture back into the bowl and set aside for about 30 minutes, stirring occasionally, until cooled to room temperature. For more rapid chilling, half-fill a sink with cold water and ice and place the bowl of mixture in it for 20 minutes. Never put the hot mixture into the fridge.

5. Once cooled, cover the mixture and refrigerate, ideally overnight, but at least for 6 hours, until thoroughly chilled (at least 4°C).

6. Carefully strain the chilled mixture through a sieve to remove the lavender, if necessary. For a stronger flavour, using a spoon, stir in the lavender honey. Pour into an ice cream machine and churn according to the manufacturer's instructions. If making by hand, see the instructions on page 15.

7. When the churning is completed, use a spoon or spatula to scrape the ice cream into a freezer-proof container with a lid. Freeze until it reaches the correct scooping texture (at least 2 hours).

8. Decorate each portion with lavender flowers before serving.

CAN YOU LICK IT? YES, YOU CAN!

MELTS HEARTS AT 50 PACES. A LOVE LETTER TO LAVENDER SOFTLY PERFUMED WITH LEMONY OVERTONES.

Inside scoop

THE LADYCHILLER
ROSE PETAL ICE CREAM

FANCY SOME HEAVY PETAL? THE DAY BEFORE WE OPENED OUR BAR IN SELFRIDGES, WE WERE MAKING OUR FIRST-EVER BATCH OF ROSE PETAL ICE CREAM FOR A PHOTO SHOOT. SOMEHOW A CATFIGHT BETWEEN TWO MODELS ESCALATED INTO AN FULL-BLOWN ICE CREAM FIGHT IN LINGERIE. GIVEN THAT OUR VIRGIN BATCH OF ICE CREAM WAS BEING THROWN, CATAPULTED AND SMEARED AROUND OUR BRAND NEW ICE CREAM BAR, I SUMMONED VAST RESERVES OF CHURCHILLIAN DETERMINATION TO SEPARATE THE TWO LADIES. AFTER SOME COVERTLY RECORDED FOOTAGE MADE IT ON TO YOUTUBE, THIS ICE CREAM BECAME AN INSTANT BEST SELLER.

· 250ml (8fl oz) full-fat milk · 125ml (4fl oz) double cream · 2 egg yolks ·
· 88g (3¼oz) caster sugar · 1 tsp vanilla extract ·
· 100ml (3½fl oz) rose water · edible rose petals, to decorate ·

1. Pour the milk and cream into a large saucepan and heat gently, stirring occasionally, until the mixture begins to steam but not boil.

2. Meanwhile, whisk the egg yolks in a heatproof bowl until smooth. Add the sugar and salt and whisk until pale and slightly fluffy. Gradually and slowly, pour the hot milk into the egg mixture whilst whisking continuously to prevent the eggs scrambling. Return the mixture to the saucepan and place over a low heat, stirring frequently until the custard thinly coats the back of a wooden spoon. Do not allow to boil.

3. Turn off the heat and whisk in the vanilla extract and rose water. Pour the mixture back into the bowl and set aside for about 30 minutes, stirring occasionally, until cooled to room temperature. For more rapid chilling, half-fill a sink with cold water and ice and place the bowl of mixture in it for 20 minutes. Never put the hot mixture into the fridge.

4. Once cooled, cover the mixture and refrigerate, ideally overnight, but at least for 6 hours, until thoroughly chilled (at least 4°C).

5. Pour the chilled mixture into an ice cream machine and churn according to the manufacturer's instructions. If making by hand, see the instructions on page 15.

6. When the churning is completed, use a spoon or spatula to scrape the ice cream into a freezer-proof container with a lid. Freeze until it reaches the correct scooping texture (at least 2 hours).

7. Decorate each portion with edible rose petals before serving.

ANY MORE CHILLED AND SHE'LL NEED GRITTING

THE FEMME FATALE OF ICE CREAMS, ITS FRAGRANT NOTES WILL TRANSPORT YOU TO A BOUDOIR AND BEYOND

Inside scoop

BABY GOOGOO
BREAST MILK ICE CREAM

TABOO OR NOT TABOO? THAT WAS THE QUESTION THE ICECREAMISTS POSED TO THE WORLD ON 25 FEBRUARY 2011, AS WE WERE ABOUT TO OPEN OUR FIRST PERMANENT ICE CREAM BOUTIQUE. THIS SIMPLE POLITICAL EXPERIMENT DIDN'T JUST CAUSE A RIPPLE, BUT A STORM IN A D CUP. FORMERLY KNOWN AS 'BABY GAGA', BEFORE LADY GAGA PUT THE SQUEEZE ON ME, WE WANTED TO ASK WHETHER IT WAS BETTER FOR US TO CONSUME THE BODILY FLUID (BOVINE JUICE) OF ANOTHER MAMMAL, OR MOTHER'S MILK, WHICH HAS WEANED HUMANITY SAFELY FOR THOUSANDS OF YEARS WITHOUT A SINGLE RECORDED DEATH. WHY DON'T YOU SUCK IT AND SEE?

- 250ml (8fl oz) free-range, organic and freshly squeezed breast milk
(the milk should be screened in line with hospital standards for blood tests)
- 125ml (4fl oz) double cream · 2 egg yolks
- 88g (3¼oz) caster sugar · pinch of sea salt · ½ vanilla pod, split lengthways

1. Pour the milk and cream into a large saucepan. Scrape in the vanilla seeds, then add the empty pod and heat gently, stirring occasionally, until the mixture begins to steam but not boil.

2. Meanwhile, whisk the egg yolks in a heatproof bowl until smooth. Add the sugar and salt and whisk until pale and slightly fluffy. Gradually and slowly, pour the hot milk into the egg mixture whilst whisking continuously to prevent the eggs scrambling. Return the mixture to the saucepan and place over a low heat, stirring frequently until the custard thinly coats the back of a wooden spoon. Do not allow to boil.

3. Pour back into the bowl and set aside for about 30 minutes, stirring occasionally, until cooled to room temperature. For more rapid chilling, half-fill a sink with cold water and ice and place the bowl of mixture in it for 20 minutes. Never put the hot mixture into the fridge.

4. Once cooled, cover the mixture and refrigerate, ideally overnight, but at least for 6 hours, until thoroughly chilled (at least 4°C).

5. Remove the vanilla pod and pour the mixture into an ice cream machine. Churn according to the manufacturer's instructions. If making by hand, see the instructions on page 15.

6. When the churning is completed, use a spoon or spatula to scrape the ice cream into a freezer-proof container with a lid. Freeze until it reaches the correct scooping texture (at least 2 hours).

ABSOLUTELY DELICIOUS AND NUTRITIOUS DAVID WALLIAMS

Inside scoop BREAST MILK IS THINNER THAN COWS' MILK AND THE FLAVOUR CAN VARY DEPENDING ON WHAT THE DONOR HAS EATEN AND HOW LONG THEY HAVE BEEN BREASTFEEDING. THE CREAM AND OTHER INGREDIENTS GIVE IT STRUCTURE AND DEPTH. IF YOU ARE COOKING FRIED PLACENTA, IT IS A GREAT DESSERT. IF NOT, MAKE IT AND MILK IT FOR ALL IT'S WORTH.

BLACK ICE
LIQUORICE ICE CREAM

AS ANYONE WHO KNOWS ME WILL TESTIFY, MY BODY IS A TEMPLE. A BUDDHIST TEMPLE. FRIENDS HAVE CRUELLY SUGGESTED I HAD BEEN IN TRAINING FOR THE FOLLOWING EVENTS IN THE LONDON 2012 OLYMPIC GAMES – THE DIABETICS AND THE PARALYTICS. IN RESPONSE, I THOUGHT I COULD KILL TWO BIRDS WITH ONE STONE BY UNDERGOING AN EIGHT-DAY HUNGER STRIKE OUTSIDE THE HOME OF THE PRIME MINISTER IN PROTEST ABOUT THE LACK OF EQUAL PARENTING RIGHTS IN THE UK. BY DAY 6, AN ARMED RESPONSE TEAM WERE PROTECTING DAVID CAMERON'S FRIDGE AND I WOULD HAVE KILLED FOR A QUICHE. I KNEW LIQUORICE HAD TO BE IN THE BOOK AFTER I BEGAN HALLUCINATING ABOUT BERTIE BASSETT. THE PRIME MINISTER SUBSEQUENTLY SENT ME A LETTER AS SLIPPERY AS HIS PRE-ELECTION COMMITMENTS.

• 75g (2½oz) **Pontefract cakes or black liquorice sticks, gently crushed** • 250ml (8fl oz) **full-fat milk**
• 125ml (4fl oz) **double cream** • 2 **egg yolks** • 88g (3¼oz) **caster sugar** • ¼ **teaspoon vanilla extract** •
few drops of natural black food colouring

1. Put the liquorice in a saucepan with 100ml (3½fl oz) water and place over a low heat for 15 minutes, stirring occasionally, until the liquorice has melted.

2. Meanwhile pour the milk and cream into a large saucepan and heat gently, stirring occasionally, until the mixture begins to steam but not boil.

3. Whisk the egg yolks in a heatproof bowl until smooth. Add the sugar and vanilla and whisk until pale and slightly fluffy. Gradually and slowly, pour the hot milk into the egg mixture whilst whisking continuously to prevent the eggs scrambling. Return the mixture to the saucepan, place over a low heat, and stir in the melted liquorice and heat until the custard thinly coats the back of a wooden spoon. Do not allow to boil. Add the black food colouring to desired effect.

4. Pour back into the bowl and set aside for about 30 minutes, stirring occasionally, until cooled to room temperature. For more rapid chilling, half-fill a sink with cold water and ice and place the bowl of mixture in it for 20 minutes. Never put the hot mixture into the fridge.

5. Once cooled, cover the mixture and refrigerate, ideally overnight, but at least for 6 hours, until thoroughly chilled (at least 4°C). Pour the chilled mixture into an ice cream machine and churn according to the manufacturer's instructions. If making by hand, see the instructions on page 15.

6. When the churning is complete, use a spoon or spatula to scrape the ice cream into a freezer-proof container with a lid. Freeze until it reaches the correct scooping texture (at least 2 hours).

DO US A FLAVOUR

Inside scoop CALABRIAN LIQUORICE IS PROBABLY THE BEST IN THE WORLD. THE SOIL AND CLIMATE IN CALABRIA, THE 'TOE' OF ITALY, IS IDEAL FOR GROWING GLYCYRRHIZA GLABRA, THE ROOTS OF WHICH PRODUCE LIQUORICE WITH A BITTER-SWEET TASTE THAT IS SAID TO HAVE SOOTHING PROPERTIES FOR DIGESTION AND SORE THROATS

LADY MARMALADE
SEVILLE MARMALADE ICE CREAM

MY FIRST WIFE WAS A ONE-WOMAN SPANISH INQUISITION. A LETHAL, LIBERIAN ASSASSIN WITH A STUTTERING GOOSE-STEP LIKE GENERAL FRANCO IN A SKIRT. BUT IT WASN'T ALL BAD. WHEN WE WERE YOUNGER SHE TRIED TO HAVE ME KILLED. IT WAS SEMANA SANTA (HOLY WEEK) IN SEVILLE. THE STREETS WERE OVERFLOWING WITH STREAMS OF HUMANITY POURING OUT ACROSS THE BARRIOS, AND THE AIR WAS FRAGRANT WITH ORANGE BLOSSOM. MY WIFE SUGGESTED WE VISIT THE SMALL TOWN OF ARCOS DE LA FRONTERA ON EASTER MORNING FOR A MARMALADE-ON-TOAST BREAKFAST AND AN INVIGORATING BULL-RUN WITH A HALF-TON OF SPANISH STEAK NUZZLING MY ARSE. I NEARLY ENDED UP AS A SPANISH KEBAB THANKS TO EL TORO, BUT SURVIVED TO TELL THE TALE. UNLIKE MY TOAST.

• 250ml (8fl oz) full-fat milk • 125ml (4fl oz) double cream • 2 egg yolks
• 88g (3¼oz) caster sugar • 135g (4½oz) Seville orange marmalade, plus extra to decorate
• zest of 1 orange

1. Pour the milk and cream into a large saucepan and heat gently, stirring occasionally, until the mixture begins to steam but not boil.

2. Meanwhile, whisk the egg yolks in a heatproof bowl until smooth. Add the sugar and whisk until pale and slightly fluffy. Gradually and slowly, pour the hot milk into the egg mixture whilst whisking continuously to prevent the eggs scrambling. Return the mixture to the saucepan and place over a low heat, stirring frequently until the custard thinly coats the back of a wooden spoon. Do not allow to boil.

3. Add the marmalade and mix with a stick blender. Pour the mixture back into the bowl and set aside for about 30 minutes, stirring occasionally, until cooled to room temperature. For more rapid chilling, half-fill a sink with cold water and ice and place the bowl of mixture in it for 20 minutes. Never put the hot mixture into the fridge.

4. Once cooled, cover the mixture and refrigerate, ideally overnight, but at least for 6 hours, until thoroughly chilled (at least 4°C). Pour the chilled mixture into an ice cream machine and churn according to the manufacturer's instructions. If making by hand, see the instructions on page 15.

5. When the churning is completed. Use a spoon or spatula to scrape the mixture into a freezer-proof container with a lid. Freeze until it reaches the correct scooping texture (at least 2 hours).

6. Decorate each portion with the orange zest and dollops of marmalade before serving.

YOU ONLY LICK TWICE

TART ANDALUSIAN ORANGE ZEST OFFSET BY A THICK, CREAMY MOUTHFEEL

Inside scoop

BORN AND BRED

BROWN BREAD AND IRISH STOUT ICE CREAM

MY IRISH CLAN HAIL FROM THE VILLAGE OF SNEEM, A JEWEL ON THE RING OF KERRY. ON A ROCKY PROMONTORY STANDS PARKNASILLA HOTEL, HISTORICAL HAVEN FOR LUMINARIES SUCH AS GEORGE BERNARD SHAW, CHARLIE CHAPLIN, CHARLES DE GAULLE AND PRINCESS GRACE OF MONACO. IT WAS THERE IN 1977, AS A SHY, STUTTERING TEN-YEAR-OLD BOY, I MET THE THEN TAOISEACH JACK LYNCH AT THE PIER BENEATH THE HOTEL. BACK AT THE BAR, HEAD BARMAN SONNY LOONEY SERVED MY FATHER A BEAUTIFULLY POURED PINT OF GUINNESS INTO WHICH I DUNKED MY RICH, BUTTERMILK-LADEN SLICE OF SODA BREAD. MY DAD LATER TOLD ME THE O'CONNORS WERE THE LAST KINGS OF IRELAND, QUITE POSSIBLY BECAUSE WE SPENT SO MUCH TIME IN THE BAR. SLÁINTE!

• 250ml (8fl oz) full-fat milk • ½ tsp allspice • ½ tsp nutmeg • 125ml (4fl oz) double cream • 2 egg yolks • 88g (3¼oz) muscovado sugar • 20g (¾oz) Irish soda bread, crumbled • 50ml (2fl oz) Irish stout (such as Guinness)

FOR THE CARAMELIZED CRUMBS • 30g (1¼oz) Irish soda bread, crumbled
• 30g (1¼oz) muscovado sugar

1. Pour the milk, spices and cream into a large saucepan and heat gently, stirring occasionally, until the mixture begins to steam but not boil.

2. Meanwhile, whisk the egg yolks in a heatproof bowl until smooth. Add the sugar and whisk until slightly fluffy. Gradually and slowly, pour the hot milk into the egg mixture whilst whisking continuously to prevent the eggs scrambling. Return the mixture to the saucepan and place over a low heat, stirring frequently until the custard thinly coats the back of a wooden spoon. Do not allow to boil.

3. Add the soda bread and mix with a stick blender, then pour the mixture back into the bowl and set aside for about 30 minutes, stirring occasionally, until cooled to room temperature. For more rapid chilling, half-fill a sink with cold water and ice and place the bowl of mixture in it for 20 minutes. Never put the hot mixture into the fridge.

4. Once cooled, boil the stout until it is reduced by about half and add to the custard. Cover the mixture and refrigerate, ideally overnight, but at least for 6 hours, until thoroughly chilled (at least 4°C). Pour the chilled mixture into an ice cream machine and churn according to the manufacturer's instructions. If making by hand, see the instructions on page 15.

5. Meanwhile prepare the topping. Combine the soda bread and sugar and spread over a shallow baking tray. Place under a medium-hot grill, stirring frequently until the breadcrumbs are softly caramelized. Allow to cool a little.

6. Fold all but 20g (¾oz) of the toasted bread mixture into the ice cream, then use a spoon or spatula to scrape the ice cream into a freezer-proof container with a lid. Freeze until it reaches the correct scooping texture (at least 2 hours).

7. Decorate each portion with a few of the remaining caramelized crumbs before serving. Enjoy with a chilled pint of Irish stout.

LIKE A THICK, PILLOWY BLANKET OF CREAM, WITH A SOFT BUTTER CRUNCH OF
BREADCRUMB AND BITTER STOUT FLAVOUR

Inside scoop

FROM ROCHER WITH LOVE

PRALINE AND CHOCOLATE ICE CREAM

A GREAT PART OF IRISH LIFE IS DEATH. AFTER MY FATHER DIED, WE FLEW HIS BODY BACK TO IRELAND. A GIRL SITTING BESIDE ME ON THE PLANE ASKED IF I WAS ALONE. 'NO,' I SAID, 'I'M WITH MY FATHER.' 'WHERE'S HE SITTING?' SHE ASKED. 'IN THE HOLD,' I SAID. 'WHAT'S HE DOING IN THE HOLD?' SHE ASKED. MY IRISH RELATIVES REFUSED POINT BLACK TO BELIEVE IN HIS MORTALITY. 'YOUR FATHER ALWAYS WAS A F*%&ING MAGICIAN,' SAID MY UNCLE NOEL. DAD WAS FOND OF CHOCOLATE, ESPECIALLY THE GOLDEN BALLS OF FERRERO ROCHER. I HOPE HE CAN STILL TASTE THIS WHEREVER HE IS IN THE UNIVERSE.

• 250ml (8fl oz) full-fat milk • 125ml (4fl oz) double cream • 2 egg yolks
• 88g (3¼oz) caster sugar • 225g (7½oz) hazelnut chocolate spread (such as Nutella) •
6 chocolate praline balls (such as Ferrero Rocher), roughly chopped • edible gold balls, to decorate

1. Pour the milk and cream into a large saucepan and heat gently, stirring occasionally, until the mixture begins to steam but not boil.

2. Meanwhile, whisk the egg yolks in a heatproof bowl until smooth. Add the sugar and whisk until pale and slightly fluffy. Gradually and slowly, pour the hot milk into the egg mixture whilst whisking continuously to prevent the eggs scrambling. Return the mixture to the saucepan and place over a low heat, stirring frequently until the custard thinly coats the back of a wooden spoon. Do not allow to boil.

3. Add 150g (5oz) of the hazelnut chocolate spread and mix with a stick blender. Pour the mixture back into the bowl and set aside for about 30 minutes, stirring occasionally, until cooled to room temperature. For more rapid chilling, half-fill a sink with cold water and ice and place the bowl of mixture in it for 20 minutes. Never put the hot mixture into the fridge.

4. Once cooled, cover the mixture and refrigerate, ideally overnight, but at least for 6 hours, until thoroughly chilled (at least 4°C). Pour into an ice cream machine and churn according to the manufacturer's instructions. If making by hand, see the instructions on page 15.

5. When the churning is completed, put the remaining 75g (2½oz) hazelnut chocolate spread in a heatproof bowl and microwave for 20 seconds on medium, or until runny. Fold into the ice cream along with the chocolate praline balls.

6. Use a spoon or spatula to scrape the ice cream into a freezer-proof container with a lid. Freeze until it reaches the correct scooping texture (at least 2 hours).

7. Chocoholics Anonymous can serve the ice cream with extra chocolate sauce (see page 154) and edible gold balls.

LICENSED TO CHILL

ACATHARTIC DOUBLE WHAMMY OF HAZELNUT CHOC SPREAD AND PRALINE WHIPPED TOGETHER INTO AN EXHILARATING STORM OF NUTTY COCOA FLAVOURS.

Inside scoop

SMACK, CRACK AND POP
POPCORN ICE CREAM

POPCORN HAS ALWAYS BEEN ONE OF THE HOLY GRAILS OF ICE CREAM BECAUSE OF ITS PROPENSITY TO SOFTEN. HOWEVER, IN THE SUMMER OF 2011 WE MADE A MIX FOR FUN AND EVERYBODY DEVOURED IT IN SECONDS. WITH ADDICTIVE PROPERTIES LIKE THIS, WE CHRISTENED IT 'SMACK, CRACK AND POP'. THIS IS AN ICE CREAM THAT'S LIKE CRACK COCAINE. IN A TUB.

· 250ml (8fl oz) full-fat milk · 125ml (4fl oz) double cream · 2 egg yolks · 88g (3¼oz) caster sugar · large pinch of sea salt · 75g (3oz) Butterkist Toffee Popcorn, plus extra for decorating · 1 handful mini butterscotch chips · 20ml (¾fl oz) Dulce de Leche Sauce, warmed (see page 154)

1. Pour the milk and cream into a large saucepan and heat gently, stirring occasionally, until the mixture begins to steam but not boil.

2. Meanwhile, whisk the egg yolks in a heatproof bowl until smooth. Add the sugar and salt and whisk until pale and slightly fluffy. Gradually and slowly, pour the hot milk into the egg mixture whilst whisking continuously to prevent the eggs scrambling. Return the mixture to the saucepan and place over a low heat, stirring frequently until the custard thinly coats the back of a wooden spoon. Do not allow to boil.

3. Add the popcorn, blend with a stick blender then sieve the custard through a strainer. Pour back into the bowl and set aside for about 30 minutes, stirring occasionally, until cooled to room temperature. For more rapid chilling, half-fill a sink with cold water and ice and place the bowl of mixture in it for 20 minutes. Never put the hot mixture into the fridge.

4. Once cooled, cover the mixture and refrigerate, ideally overnight, but at least for 6 hours, until thoroughly chilled (at least 4°C). Pour the chilled mixture into an ice cream machine and churn according to the manufacturer's instructions. If making by hand, see the instructions on page 15.

5. When the churning is completed, fold a handful (or as many as you want) of the butterscotch chips into the ice cream. Use a spoon or spatula to scrape it into a freezer-proof container with a lid. Freeze until it reaches the correct scooping texture (at least 2 hours).

6. Drizzle each portion with a little warmed sauce and decorate with the extra popcorn before serving.

GIMME SOME SUGAR, BABY BRUCE CAMPBELL, ARMY OF DARKNESS

HIGHLY ADDICTIVE CHEWY CARAMEL NOTES FOLLOWED BY CRUNCHY BUTTERSCOTCH PIECES AND POPCORN BITES. THIS IS POP-TRASH ICE CREAM AT ITS FINEST.

Inside scoop

THE MICHELIN MAN
MARSHMALLOW ICE CREAM

AT THE ICECREAMISTS WE SAY, 'MARSHMALLOW MAKETH THE MAN'. AS SOMEONE SUFFERING FROM OCCASIONAL BOUTS OF WARDROBE DYSFUNCTION, I CAN REGULARLY BE SEEN ON GOOGLE EARTH WEARING SOME COLOURFUL GARMENTS THAT ACCOMODATE A MAN WHOSE SIZE REFLECTS HIS DEDICATION TO HIS ART. IN A PREVIOUS LIFE, I WAS AFFLICTED BY A FASCINATION FOR LYCRA SUPER-SUITS, BROUGHT TO NATIONAL ATTENTION DURING MY CAMPAIGNING DAYS. FEW PEOPLE WILL SYMPATHIZE WITH THE PITFALLS OF WEARING TIGHT, STRETCHY POLYESTER GARMENTS AND SUPERHERO GARB, BUT THE CHANCES ARE THAT YOU WILL LOOK MORE LIKE THE MICHELIN MAN THAN SUPERMAN, WITH PILLOWY EXPANSES OF MARSHMALLOW EXPANDING INTO PLACES WHERE NO LYCRA HAS EVER GONE BEFORE.

- 250ml (8fl oz) full-fat milk · 125ml (4fl oz) double cream · 2 egg yolks
- 88g (3¾oz) caster sugar · 100g (3½oz) large marshmallows
- a few small marshmallows, to decorate

FOR THE RIPPLE · 50g (2 oz) small mixed marshmallows
- 100g (3½oz) Marshmallow Fluff (Crème)

1. Pour the milk and cream into a large saucepan and heat gently, stirring occasionally, until the mixture begins to steam but not boil.

2. Meanwhile, whisk the egg yolks in a heatproof bowl until smooth. Add the sugar and whisk until pale and slightly fluffy. Gradually and slowly, pour the hot milk into the egg mixture whilst whisking continuously to prevent the eggs scrambling. Return the mixture to the saucepan and place over a low heat, stirring frequently until the custard thinly coats the back of a wooden spoon. Do not allow to boil.

3. Stir the large marshmallows into the warm custard until melted. Pour back into the bowl and set aside for about 30 minutes, stirring occasionally, until cooled to room temperature. For more rapid chilling, half-fill a sink with cold water and ice and place the bowl of mixture in it for 20 minutes. Never put the hot mixture into the fridge.

4. Once cooled, cover the mixture and refrigerate, ideally overnight, but at least for 6 hours, until thoroughly chilled (at least 4°C). Pour the chilled mixture into an ice cream machine and churn according to the manufacturer's instructions. If making by hand, see the instructions on page 15.

5. When the churning is completed, fold in the small marshmallows and Marshmallow Fluff. Use a spoon or spatula to scrape the ice cream into a freezer-proof container with a lid. Freeze until it reaches the correct scooping texture (at least 2 hours).

6. Decorate each portion with a few small marshmallows before serving.

RELEASE YOUR INNER CHILD WITH THIS FLUFFY REMAKE OF THE OLD TUCK SHOP FAVOURITE

Inside scoop

THE CAKED CRUSADER

JAMAICAN GINGER CAKE ICE CREAM

MY LATE BUSINESS PARTNER, PETER MATTHEWS, WAS AN ENTREPRENEUR WITH A CARROT TOP, SCHOOLBOYISH WIT AND EXTRAORDINARY ENERGY. PETER MATTHEWS' PARTIES WERE THE STUFF OF LEGEND, AND HE WAS FOREVER GETTING EMBROILED IN NEAR-DEATH YET LIFE-AFFIRMING EXPERIENCES THAT ENCOURAGED HIM TO PURSUE EVER MORE RECKLESS BEHAVIOUR. WHEN HE WAS REPORTED DEAD IN AN ACCIDENT ABROAD, ONE COULDN'T HELP BUT THINK HE HAD FAKED HIS OWN DEMISE IN AN ATTEMPT TO EVADE THE TAX INSPECTOR. I IMAGINE HE IS NOW RESIDING UNDER A VARIETY OF NOMS DE PLUME. BEING A GINGER, HE WAS PARTIAL TO A BIT OF THIS CAKE, SO THIS ONE IS FOR PETER, WHEREVER YOU ARE...

• 250ml (8fl oz) full-fat milk • 125ml (4fl oz) double cream • 2 egg yolks • 88g (3¼oz) caster sugar
• 1 heaped tsp ground ginger, plus extra for dusting • 1 Jamaican Ginger Cake • 2 balls of stem ginger, chopped
• slug of stem ginger syrup • dark rum, to serve (optional)

FOR THE SUGAR SYRUP • 75g (3oz) caster sugar • 75ml (3fl oz) water

1. Pour the milk and cream into a large saucepan and heat gently, stirring occasionally, until the mixture begins to steam but not boil.

2. Meanwhile, whisk the egg yolks in a heatproof bowl until smooth. Add the caster sugar and whisk until pale and slightly fluffy. Gradually and slowly, pour the hot milk into the egg mixture whilst whisking continuously to prevent the eggs scrambling. Return the mixture to the saucepan, add the ground ginger and place over a low heat, stirring frequently until the custard thinly coats the back of a wooden spoon. Do not allow to boil.

3. Pour back into the bowl and set aside for about 30 minutes, stirring occasionally, until cooled to room temperature. For more rapid chilling, half-fill a sink with cold water and ice and place the bowl of mixture in it for 20 minutes. Never put the hot mixture into the fridge.

4. When chilled, add 90g (3¼oz) of the cake, the stem ginger and syrup and blend until smooth. Cover and refrigerate, ideally overnight, but at least for 6 hours, until thoroughly chilled (at least 4°C). Pour the chilled mixture into an ice cream machine and churn according to the manufacturer's instructions. If making by hand, see the instructions on page 15.

5. When the churning is completed, prepare the sugar syrup by putting the sugar and water in a saucepan over a medium heat and stirring until the sugar dissolves. Allow to simmer for a few minutes, until the liquid becomes a syrup.

6. Thinly slice the remaining cake and drizzle the sugar syrup over it until damp, but not saturated. Fold the cake through the ice cream, then scrape into a freezer-proof container with a lid. Freeze until it reaches the correct scooping texture (at least 2 hours). For an extra kick, dust each portion with a little more ground ginger, or add a slug of dark rum before serving.

COOLING CREAM RIPPLED WITH RICH, MOIST CAKE AND A PENETRATING KICK LIKE A GINGER JAVELIN

Inside scoop

THE BAIL-OUT

IRISH CREAM LIQUEUR AND BRANDY ICE CREAM

JULIE WAS THE BEWITCHING IRISH TEMPTRESS AT THE HORSESHOE BAR OF THE SHELBOURNE HOTEL, DUBLIN, WHO INTRODUCED ME TO THIS MILITARILY UPGRADED VERSION OF BAILEYS, FUEL-INJECTED WITH A DOUBLE SHOT OF BRANDY. IN 2005, WHEN MRS O' AND I ENJOYED A FILTHY WEEKEND IN BRIGHTON, THE AFTERNOON WAS LOST CONSUMING DOUBLE BAILEYS AND BRANDY. BRIGHTON CERTAINLY ROCKED BECAUSE NINE MONTHS LATER WE HAD ANOTHER SOUVENIR TO GO WITH THE KISS ME QUICK HAT AND STICK OF BRIGHTON ROCK – OUR SON ARCHIE.

· 250ml (8fl oz) full-fat milk · 125ml (4fl oz) double cream · 2 egg yolks
· 88g (3¼oz) caster sugar · 50ml (2fl oz) Irish Cream liqueur (such as Baileys), plus extra to serve
· 2 tsp brandy

1. Pour the milk and cream into a large saucepan and heat gently, stirring occasionally, until the mixture begins to steam but not boil.

2. Meanwhile, whisk the egg yolks in a heatproof bowl until smooth. Add the sugar and whisk until pale and slightly fluffy. Gradually and slowly, pour the hot milk into the egg mixture whilst whisking continuously to prevent the eggs scrambling. Return the mixture to the saucepan and place over a low heat, stirring frequently until the custard thinly coats the back of a wooden spoon. Do not allow to boil.

3. Stir in the Irish cream liqueur and brandy, then pour the mixture back into the bowl and set aside for about 30 minutes, stirring occasionally, until cooled to room temperature. For more rapid chilling, half-fill a sink with cold water and ice and place the bowl of mixture in it for 20 minutes. Never put the hot mixture into the fridge.

4. Once cooled, cover the mixture and refrigerate, ideally overnight, but at least for 6 hours, until thoroughly chilled (at least 4°C). Pour the chilled mixture into an ice cream machine and churn according to the manufacturer's instructions. If making by hand, see the instructions on page 15.

5. When the churning is completed, use a spoon or spatula to scrape the ice cream into a freezer-proof container with a lid. Freeze until it reaches the correct scooping texture (at least 2 hours).

6. Pour a little extra Baileys on each portion before serving.

YOU CAN ENJOY ICECREAMISM ANYWHERE: AGAINST THE BAR, AGAINST THE WALL AND AGAINST THE LAW

LIKE A BREATHLESS IRISH BANSHEE – DECADENT AND CREAMY WITH AN UNEXPECTED CELTIC KICK

Inside scoop

DOUGHNUT STOP BELIEVIN'

JAMMY DOUGHNUT ICE CREAM

WHY IS IT THAT AS SOON AS THE GOVERNMENT SEES ANYBODY ENJOYING SOMETHING THEY WANT TO TAX IT? WHEN WE HEARD ABOUT THE 'FAT TAX' WE WENT WHERE NO RESPONSIBLE ICE CREAM MAN HAD GONE BEFORE AND CAME UP WITH THE IDEA OF THE 'DOH-LYMPICS'. SCOFF YOUR WAY THROUGH 5 DOUGHNUT RINGS AND 2012 CALORIES PER PORTION OF THE WORLD'S FATTEST ICE CREAM. OUR OLYMPIC MOTTO 'SLOWER, LOWER, FATTER'.

· 250ml (8fl oz) full-fat milk · 1 tsp ground cinnamon · 125ml (4fl oz) double cream · 2 egg yolks · 88g (3¼oz) caster sugar · 2 plain ring doughnuts · a few fresh raspberries, to decorate

FOR THE RIPPLE · 75g (3oz) raspberry jam · 30g (1¼oz) fresh raspberries · 75g (3oz) caster sugar · 75ml (3fl oz) water · 2 ring doughnuts, chopped into bite-sized pieces

1. Pour the milk, cinnamon and cream into a large saucepan and heat gently, stirring occasionally, until the mixture begins to steam but not boil.

2. Meanwhile, whisk the egg yolks in a heatproof bowl until smooth. Add the sugar and whisk until pale and slightly fluffy. Gradually and slowly, pour the hot milk into the egg mixture whilst whisking continuously to prevent the eggs scrambling. Return the mixture to the saucepan and place over a low heat, stirring frequently until the custard thinly coats the back of a wooden spoon. Do not allow to boil.

3. Blend the doughnuts into the warm custard using a stick blender until the mixture is smooth. Pour back into the bowl and set aside for about 30 minutes, stirring occasionally, until cooled to room temperature. For more rapid chilling, half-fill a sink with cold water and ice and place the bowl of mixture in it for 20 minutes. Never put the hot mixture into the fridge.

4. Once cooled, cover the mixture and refrigerate, ideally overnight, but at least for 6 hours, until thoroughly chilled (at least 4°C). Pour the chilled mixture into an ice cream machine and churn according to the manufacturer's instructions. If making by hand, see the instructions on page 15.

5. When the churning is completed, prepare the ripple by mashing the jam and raspberries together with a fork. Set aside.

6. Place the sugar and water in a saucepan over a medium heat and stir until the sugar dissolves. Allow to simmer for a few minutes, until the liquid becomes a syrup. Put the doughnut pieces into the syrup until lightly soaked, but not saturated or falling apart. Fold into the ice cream along with the raspberry mixture. Use a spoon or spatula to scrape the ice cream into a freezer-proof container with a lid. Freeze until it reaches the correct scooping texture (at least 2 hours).

7. Decorate each portion with few raspberries before serving.

Inside scoop

THIS IS AN ICE CREAM THAT IS FULL FAT AND GETTING FATTER. TO CUT THROUGH THE ARTERY-CLOGGING CALORIES, IT'S RIPPLED WITH JAM AND FRESH, TART RASPBERRIES, WHICH WILL DELAY THE ONSET OF A CORONARY LONG ENOUGH FOR YOU TO SINK A FEW EXTRA SCOOPS.

COMPLETELY PEANUTS
PEANUT BUTTER ICE CREAM

I ALWAYS WONDERED WHY REHAB WAS SO EXPENSIVE – YOU WENT IN WITH ONE ADDICTION AND LEFT WITH FOUR. AFTER GROUP SEX, ALCOHOL SMUGGLING AND GAMBLING ADDICTION, PEANUT BUTTER SANDWICHES CAME AS SOMETHING OF AN ANTI-CLIMAX. I WASN'T A HUGE FAN, BUT IN REHAB IT WAS THE DRUG DU JOUR – ON TOAST. AFTER MY SECOND SLICE, I UNDERWENT A DAMASCENE CONVERSION AND BECAME A BORN-AGAIN PEANUT BUTTER BELIEVER. DURING MY SUBSEQUENT 'SHARE', I TOLD THEM THAT REHAB WAS FOR QUITTERS AND MY HIGHER POWER HAD REVEALED ITSELF IN THE SHAPE OF PEANUT BUTTER ICE CREAM.

- 250ml (8fl oz) full-fat milk • 125ml (4fl oz) double cream • 2 egg yolks
- 88g (3¼oz) caster sugar • large pinch of sea salt • 250g (8oz) peanut butter
- 25g (1oz) unsalted peanuts, chopped, plus a few extra to decorate • brioche slices

1. Pour the milk and cream into a large saucepan and heat gently, stirring occasionally, until the mixture begins to steam but not boil.

2. Meanwhile, whisk the egg yolks in a heatproof bowl until smooth. Add the sugar and whisk until pale and slightly fluffy. Gradually and slowly, pour the hot milk into the egg mixture whilst whisking continuously to prevent the eggs scrambling. Return the mixture to the saucepan and place over a low heat, stirring frequently until the custard thinly coats the back of a wooden spoon. Do not allow to boil.

3. Pour back into the bowl and set aside for about 30 minutes, stirring occasionally, until cooled to room temperature. For more rapid chilling, half-fill a sink with cold water and ice and place the bowl of mixture in it for 20 minutes. Never put the hot mixture into the fridge.

4. Once cooled, cover the mixture and refrigerate, ideally overnight, but at least for 6 hours, until thoroughly chilled (at least 4°C).

5. Blend in 150g (5oz) of the peanut butter using a stick blender, then pour the mixture into an ice cream machine and churn according to manufacturer's instructions. If making by hand, see the instructions on page 15.

6. When the churning is completed, put the remaining peanut butter into a heatproof dish and microwave on medium in 20-second bursts until warm but not hot. Fold into the ice cream along with the chopped peanuts. Use a spoon or spatula to scrape the ice cream into a freezer-proof container with a lid. Freeze until it reaches the correct scooping texture (at least 2 hours).

7. Decorate each serving with a few peanuts blitzed in a blender and serve on toasted brioche slices.

MIND YOUR INNER CHILD

THERE IS NO ANTIDOTE FOR THIS NUT-CRACKING CRESCENDO OF PEANUT BUTTER MADNESS AND THICK, VELVETY WAVES OF ICE CREAM

Inside scoop

COLD SWEAT

CHILLI, GINGER AND LEMONGRASS ICE CREAM

MELT INTO THE PARADOX OF THE HOTTEST ICE CREAM ON EARTH. A SELF-IMMOLATING FIREBALL OF MIXED CHILLIES, FRESH GINGER AND LEMONGRASS HOT LICKS, OFFSET WITH THE COOLING POWER OF FRESHLY MADE GELATO. WHEN LIT, STAND WELL BACK AND ENSURE ALL WOMEN, CHILDREN AND PETS ARE KEPT INSIDE.

• 250ml (8fl oz) full-fat milk • 125ml (4fl oz) double cream • 2 egg yolks
• 88g (3¼oz) caster sugar • pinch of sea salt • 1 red chilli, deseeded and finely chopped •
thumb-size piece of fresh ginger, peeled and roughly grated
• 1 stick of lemongrass finely chopped • chilli oil, to serve

1. Pour the milk and cream into a large saucepan and heat gently, stirring occasionally, until the mixture begins to steam but not boil.

2. Meanwhile, whisk the egg yolks in a heatproof bowl until smooth. Add the sugar and whisk until pale and slightly fluffy. Gradually and slowly, pour the hot milk into the egg mixture whilst whisking continuously to prevent the eggs scrambling. Return the mixture to the saucepan and place over a low heat, stirring frequently until the custard thinly coats the back of a wooden spoon. Do not allow to boil.

3. Add the chilli, ginger and lemongrass to the custard and blend until smooth. Sieve twice through a strainer or muslin cloth to remove all fibres and seeds. Pour back into the bowl and set aside for about 30 minutes, stirring occasionally, until cooled to room temperature. For more rapid chilling, half-fill a sink with cold water and ice and place the bowl of mixture in it for 20 minutes. Never put the hot mixture into the fridge.

4. Once cooled, cover the mixture and refrigerate, ideally overnight, but at least for 6 hours, until thoroughly chilled (at least 4°C). Pour the chilled mixture into an ice cream machine and churn according to the manufacturer's instructions. If making by hand, see the instructions on page 15.

5. When the churning is completed, use a spoon or spatula to scrape the ice cream into a freezer-proof container with a lid. Freeze until it reaches the correct scooping texture (at least 2 hours). Serve in cones.

6. Drizzle each portion with chilli oil before serving.

EMERGENCY COLD RELIEF

THIS IS A MASOCHISTIC TRIPLE WHAMMY OF SWEET, SAVOURY AND SPICY FLAVOURS. AN ICE CREAM THAT WILL BOMB, BURN AND FLAME YOUR MOUTH INTO SUBMISSION BEFORE TASERING YOU INTO BLISSFUL PARALYSIS. UPGRADE YOUR SPRINKLER SYSTEM BEFORE CONSUMING.

Inside scoop

RUMBLE IN THE JUNGLE
HOT BUTTERED RUM AND RAISIN ICE CREAM

THIS IS A RECIPE THAT FLOATS LIKE A BUTTERFLY AND STINGS LIKE A BEE. TO PARAPHRASE THE LEGENDARY BOXER MUHAMMAD ALI HIMSELF, 'YOUR LIPS CAN'T LICK WHAT YOUR EYES CAN'T SEE.' IN ANYONE'S LANGUAGE, IT'S A KNOCK OUT. OUR ROCKET-FUELLED VERSION OF A TRADITIONAL RUM AND RAISIN ICE CREAM CONTAINS RUM-LACED RAISINS THAT DELIVER A DISORIENTATING RIGHT-HAND LEAD PUNCH, FOLLOWED BY A COUPLE OF SHARP, JUICY JABS. IT HAS AN EXTRA ZAP OF SAILOR JERRY SPICED RUM, BEFORE BEING COUNTED OUT WITH A HOT BUTTERED RUM SAUCE.

· 100g (3½oz) raisins · 2 slugs of Sailor Jerry Spiced Rum, or similar good-quality rum
· 250ml (8fl oz) full-fat milk · 125ml (4fl oz) double cream · ½ vanilla pod, split lengthways
· 2 egg yolks · 88g (3¼oz) muscovado sugar

FOR THE HOT BUTTERED RUM SAUCE · 88g (3¼oz) unsalted butter · 50g (2oz) muscovado sugar
· 25ml (1fl oz) double cream · 1 tbsp corn syrup · slug of Sailor Jerry Spiced Rum, or similar good-quality rum

1. Soak the raisins in a slug of rum overnight, or for a minimum of 6 hours.

2. Pour the milk and cream into a large saucepan, scrape in the vanilla seeds, then add the empty pod and heat gently, stirring occasionally, until the mixture begins to steam but not boil.

3. Meanwhile, whisk the egg yolks in a heatproof bowl until smooth. Add the sugar and whisk until slightly fluffy. Gradually and slowly, pour the hot milk into the egg mixture whilst whisking continuously to prevent the eggs scrambling. Return the mixture to the saucepan and place over a low heat, stirring frequently until the custard thinly coats the back of a wooden spoon. Do not allow to boil.

4. Pour back into the bowl and set aside for about 30 minutes, stirring occasionally, until cooled to room temperature. For more rapid chilling, half-fill a sink with cold water and ice and place the bowl of mixture in it for 20 minutes. Never put the hot mixture into the fridge.

5. Once the custard is chilled, remove the vanilla pod, then stir in the raisins and their soaking liquid, and add an extra slug of rum for good measure. Pour into an ice cream machine and churn according to manufacturer's instructions. If making by hand, see the instructions on page 15.

6. When the churning is completed, use a spoon or spatula to scrape the ice cream into a freezer-proof container with a lid. Freeze until it reaches the correct scooping texture (at least 2 hours).

7. To make the sauce, melt the butter in a saucepan over a medium heat. Add the sugar, cream and corn syrup and mix until the sugar has dissolved. Simmer until the sauce has thickened, then remove from heat and stir in a slug of rum. Pour some of the hot sauce over each serving of ice cream.

A SWAGGERING REINVENTION OF A CLASSIC FOR DIE-HARD SEA SALTS, WHICH PUNCHES ABOVE ITS WEIGHT. AN EXTRA LICK OF SPICED RUM GIVES THIS ICE CREAM ITS 'RAISIN D'ÊTRE'.

Inside scoop

SEX BOMB

STIMULANT ICE CREAM

THE ICE CREAM THE AUTHORITIES COULDN'T DEFUSE. ORIGINALLY CALLED THE SEX PISTOL DURING OUR TWO-MONTH GUERRILLA ICE CREAM POP-UP IN SELFRIDGES IN 2009, THIS WAS THE FIRST OF OUR SHOCK 'N' ROLL ICE CREAMS. LACED WITH ENOUGH ERECTILE PROPERTIES TO BRING PEOPLE BACK FROM THE DEAD, IT INCURRED THE WRATH OF JOHNNY ROTTEN, THE SEX PISTOLS, LIVE NATION AND A PHARMA GIANT. ON THE STRENGTH OF THIS, THE PROPRIETOR OF SELFRIDGES, GALEN WESTON, FLEW IN FROM CANADA TO TRY THE MEDICATION FOR HIMSELF.

· 250ml (8fl oz) full-fat milk · 125ml (4fl oz) double cream · 2 egg yolks
· 88g (3¼oz) caster sugar · 3 drops each of ginkgo biloba, arginine and guarana
· juice of 1 lemon · grated zest of ½ a lemon, plus extra to decorate

1. Pour the milk and cream into a large saucepan and heat gently, stirring occasionally, until the mixture begins to steam but not boil.

2. Meanwhile, whisk the egg yolks in a heatproof bowl until smooth. Add the sugar and whisk until pale and slightly fluffy. Gradually and slowly, pour the hot milk into the egg mixture whilst whisking continuously to prevent the eggs scrambling. Return the mixture to the saucepan and place over a low heat, stirring frequently until the custard thinly coats the back of a wooden spoon. Do not allow to boil.

3. Pour back into the bowl and set aside for about 30 minutes, stirring occasionally, until cooled to room temperature. For more rapid chilling, half-fill a sink with cold water and ice and place the bowl of mixture in it for 20 minutes. Never put the hot mixture into the fridge. Once cooled, cover the mixture and refrigerate, ideally overnight, but at least for 6 hours, until thoroughly chilled (at least 4°C).

4. Add the ginkgo, arginine, guarana, lemon juice and zest to the chilled mixture and whisk well. Pour into an ice cream machine and churn according to the manufacturer's instructions. If making by hand, see the instructions on page 15.

5. When the churning is completed, use a spoon or spatula to scrape the ice cream into a freezer-proof container with a lid. Freeze until it reaches the correct scooping texture (at least 2 hours).

6. Decorate each portion with little extra lemon zest before serving.

BUY THE TICKET, TAKE THE RIDE HUNTER S. THOMPSON

Inside scoop

CLASSIC ITALIAN FIOR DI LATTE ICE CREAM WITH A GENTLE LEMON SYLLABUB AND CITRUS ZEST INFUSION. LACED WITH NATURAL STIMULANTS FOR ENHANCED PERFORMANCE.

USED IN ≫

THE ABOMINABULL SNOWMAN

PG 130

ALEXANDER McCREAM

SPICED PUMPKIN ICE CREAM

FOR HALLOWEEN WE ATTEMPTED TO BREAK THE RECORD FOR THE WORLD'S LOUDEST SCREAM – THE ACKNOWLEDGED 'SCREAM OF ICE CREAM'. TO COINCIDE WITH THE ATTEMPT WE CREATED THE WORLD'S FIRST 'ICE CREAM SOUP', A BOWL OF STEAMING HOT PUMPKIN SOUP WITH A SCOOP OF PUMPKIN ICE CREAM DROPPED IN THE MIDDLE. I LOVED IT, BUT IT LEFT EVERYONE ELSE IN MELTDOWN. IN THE END WE RAN OUT OF TIME TO STAGE THE WORLD RECORD ATTEMPT, AND KILLED OFF ICE CREAM SOUP, BUT WE KEPT SPICED PUMPKIN ICE CREAM ALIVE.

• 250ml (8fl oz) full-fat milk • 125ml (4fl oz) double cream • 2 egg yolks
• 115g (3¾oz) caster sugar • 100g (3½oz) canned pumpkin
• ½ tsp ground cinnamon, plus extra for dusting • drop of vanilla extract
• dash of dark rum (optional)

1. Pour the milk and cream into a large saucepan and heat gently, stirring occasionally, until the mixture begins to steam but not boil.

2. Meanwhile, whisk the egg yolks in a heatproof bowl until smooth. Add 88g (3¼oz) of the sugar and whisk until pale and slightly fluffy. Gradually and slowly, pour the hot milk into the egg mixture whilst whisking continuously to prevent the eggs scrambling. Return the mixture to the saucepan and place over a low heat, stirring frequently until the custard thinly coats the back of a wooden spoon. Do not allow to boil.

3. Pour back into the bowl and set aside for about 30 minutes, stirring occasionally, until cooled to room temperature. For more rapid chilling, half-fill a sink with cold water and ice and place the bowl of mixture in it for 20 minutes. Never put the hot mixture into the fridge.

4. Put the pumpkin, cinnamon, vanilla extract, remaining sugar and a dash of rum, if using, into a blender or food processor and blend until smooth. Add to the chilled custard and whisk well. Pour the mixture into an ice cream machine and churn according to the manufacturer's instructions. If making by hand, see the instructions on page 15.

5. When the churning is completed, use a spoon or spatula to scrape the ice cream into a freezer-proof container with a lid. Freeze until it reaches the correct scooping texture (at least 2 hours). Dust each portion with a little ground cinnamon before serving.

THE DEVIL HAS ALL THE BEST LICKS

TAKE A TRIP TO THE DARK SIDE WITH THIS CUT-THROAT LICK OF AUTUMNAL FLAVOURS

Inside scoop

SORBE

SORBETTOS

THE SECRET TO SURVIVING A MODERN MELTDOWN (FINANCIAL, ECONOMIC, MARITAL) IS TO BREAK THE ICE AND REACH FOR SOME EMERGENCY COLD RELIEF. WE PRESCRIBE MOUTH-WATERING SORBETTOS AS THE MEDICATION FOR YOUR DESPERATION. THE THAWNICATING THRILLS OF AN INSPIRED SORBETTO ARE A LOOSE COMBINATION OF FLAVOURS, COLD-FUSED IN THE CRYOGENIC REACTOR OF WHITE ALCHEMY. SORBETTO IS AN ELEMENTAL FORCE OF NATURE, EMPLOYING A HOLY TRINITY OF FRESH SEASONAL FRUITS, SUGAR AND WATER TO DELIVER A BLITZKRIEG OF INCENDIARY KILLER FRUIT FLAVOURS. A CLASSIC SORBETTO WILL TASTE LIKE FRESH FRUIT MELTING IN YOUR MOUTH, AND FOR AN ADDITIONAL VISCERAL SMACK TO THE CHOPS, CHOOSE FROM LACED SORBETTOS AND FUEL-INJECT WITH AN ETHANOL SHOT OF YOUR CHOICE.

NOTE: ALL THE RECIPES IN THIS CHAPTER TAKE 15 MINUTES FOR THE BASE MIX, 6–24 HOURS FOR CHILLING, AND 20–60 MINUTES FOR CHURNING. THE RECIPES ALL MAKE AROUND 500ML (17FL OZ), WHICH WILL SERVE FOUR PEOPLE, AND ARE BEST ENJOYED WITHIN A FEW DAYS OF MAKING. AS ALL FRUIT VARIES IN FLAVOUR AND SWEETNESS, ADJUST THE RECIPES TO TASTE BEFORE YOU FREEZE YOUR SORBETTO MIX. TOP TIP: YOU CAN USE ANY OF THESE SORBETTOS TO MAKE GREAT LOLLIES.

LEMONY OF THE STATE
LEMON SORBETTO

AS ANY SELF-RESPECTING ICECREAMIST WILL TELL YOU
WHEN TALKING ABOUT A GREAT LEMON SORBETTO, IT DON'T MEAN
A THING IF IT AIN'T GOT THAT ZING. SHARP AS SARCASM, SWEET AS A
KISS, THIS TIMELESS CLASSIC IS FULL OF ZEST AND BOUNCE. ENJOY!

- 200ml (7fl oz) water • 200g (7oz) caster sugar
- 150ml (5fl oz) freshly squeezed lemon juice (about 4 lemons)
- 1 heaped tsp grated lemon zest, plus extra to decorate

1. Pour the water into a saucepan and add the sugar. Place over a low heat and bring to the boil, whisking often, until the sugar dissolves. Reduce the heat and allow to simmer for 5 minutes, continuing to whisk until the liquid turns into a syrup.

2. Pour the syrup into a heatproof bowl and set aside for about 30 minutes, stirring occasionally, until cooled to room temperature. For more rapid chilling, half-fill a sink with cold water and ice and place the bowl of mixture in it for 20 minutes.

3. Add the lemon juice to the syrup and mix with a stick blender. Cover and refrigerate, ideally overnight, until thoroughly chilled (at least 4°C).

4. Pour the chilled mixture into an ice cream machine and churn according to manufacturer's instructions. If making by hand, see the instructions on page 000.

5. When the churning is completed, use a spoon or spatula to scrape the sorbetto into a freezer-proof container with a lid. Freeze until it reaches the correct scooping texture (at least 2–3 hours).

6. Decorate each portion with a pinch of lemon zest before serving.

ORIGINAL COLD WARRIORS – ACCEPT NO IMITATIONS

Inside scoop A WONDERFULLY BALANCED SORBETTO WITH INVIGORATING LEMON FLAVOURS AND CITRUS NOTES. THE ZEST ADDS AN INTERESTING TEXTURE. IF THIS SORBETTO WERE ANY COOLER, YOU'D BE SUFFERING FROM EARLY ONSET HYPOTHERMIA.

EASYSLIDER
ELDERFLOWER SORBETTO

THE AUTHOR WILL SELF ONCE BASED A BOOK OF FICTIONAL MUSINGS UPON HIS CAPOTE-ESQUE IMPRESSION OF MY CHARACTER. BACK IN 2007 SELF HAD DROPPED BY TO INTERVIEW ME FOR A MAGAZINE AND 'FESSED UP THAT HE'D CONSTRUCTED HIS FABLE AROUND A CARICATURE HE HAD OF ME IN HIS MIND'S EYE. DESPITE THE DELIBERATE MISREPRESENTATION, I FOUND SELF TO BE AN ADMIRABLE CHAP STEEPED IN A HUMANITY ACCUMULATED WHILE BATTLING SOME PRETTY MONSTROUS DEMONS. AS WE SWAPPED INCREASINGLY DEPRAVED AND DEBAUCHED STORIES, HE SUGGESTED THAT ELDERFLOWER CORDIAL MIGHT BE THE PERFECT TONIC FOR THOSE OF US WITH A PROPENSITY FOR OVER-INDULGENCE.

- 300ml (½ pint) water · 75g (3oz) caster sugar
- 8 tbsp elderflower cordial, plus extra for drizzling
- juice of 1 lemon · sprigs of mint, to decorate

1. Pour the water into a saucepan and add the sugar. Place over a low heat and bring to the boil, whisking often, until the sugar dissolves. Reduce the heat and allow to simmer for 5 minutes, continuing to whisk until the liquid turns into a syrup.

2. Pour the syrup into a heatproof bowl and set aside for about 30 minutes, stirring occasionally, until cooled to room temperature. For more rapid chilling, half-fill a sink with cold water and ice and place the bowl of mixture in it for 20 minutes.

3. Whisk the cordial and lemon juice into the syrup. Cover and refrigerate, ideally overnight, until thoroughly chilled (at least 4°C).

4. Pour the chilled mixture into an ice cream machine and churn according to the manufacturer's instructions. If making by hand, see the instructions on page 000.

5. When the churning is completed, use a spoon or spatula to scrape the sorbetto into a freezer-proof container with a lid. Freeze until it reaches the correct scooping texture (at least 2–3 hours).

6. Drizzle a little elderflower cordial over each portion and finish with a sprig of mint before serving.

WONDERFULLY INVIGORATING HERBAL FLAVOURS OFFSET WITH SOME TART NOTES
AND A SWEET FINISH. THE ULTIMATE SUMMER SORBETTO.

Inside scoop

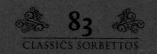

GLASTONBERRY
SEASONAL BERRY SORBETTO

DURING OUR FIRST GIG AT SELFRIDGES, BACK IN 2009, WE WHIPPED UP A MIX OF MERCURIAL MADNESS THAT WOULDN'T HAVE BEEN OUT OF PLACE AT GLASTONBURY, HOME OF THE MYSTERIOUS TOR (TOWER) AND THE FAMOUS MUSIC FESTIVAL. PROPOSED EVENTS INCLUDED THE WORLD'S FIRST INTERNATIONAL ICE CREAM WRESTLING CHAMPIONSHIPS, EXPLODING ICE CREAM VANS AND A MAN ENTOMBED IN JELLY FOR A WEEK – THE SO-CALLED 'JELLYMANJARO'. CREATING OUR FIRST SORBETTO WAS A FAR SIMPLER PROPOSITION. 'GLASTONBERRY' IS A MESMERIZING MIX OF SEASONAL BERRY SORBETTO OVERLOADED WITH LOW-HANGING, THROBBING FRUITY RIFFS AND FUEL-INJECTED WITH A SPLASH OF SOMETHING NAUGHTY.

· 120ml (3¾fl oz) water · 120g (3¾oz) caster sugar · 650g (1¼lb) fresh or frozen summer fruits (raspberries, strawberries, blueberries, etc.), sieved if frozen · juice of 1 lemon · shot of raspberry cordial · dash of grenadine (optional) · dash of aged balsamic vinegar (optional)

1. Pour the water into a saucepan and add the sugar. Place over a low heat and bring to the boil, whisking often, until the sugar dissolves. Add the summer fruits, reduce the heat and allow to simmer for 10 minutes, continuing to whisk until the liquid turns into a syrup.

2. Pour the syrup into a heatproof bowl and set aside for about 30 minutes, stirring occasionally, until cooled to room temperature. For more rapid chilling, half-fill a sink with cold water and ice and place the bowl of mixture in it for 20 minutes.

3. Add the lemon juice and shot of raspberry cordial, then sieve the mixture carefully to remove any pulp and seeds. You'll be left with a thick, rich liquid. If you'd like to spice up your sorbetto, add a dash of grenadine and aged balsamic vinegar now. Cover and refrigerate, ideally overnight, until thoroughly chilled (at least 4°C).

4. Pour the chilled mixture into an ice cream machine and churn according to the manufacturer's instructions. If making by hand, see the instructions on page 000.

5. When the churning is completed, use a spoon or spatula to scrape the sorbetto into a freezer-proof container with a lid. Freeze until it reaches the correct scooping texture (at least 2–3 hours).

MAKE ICE CREAM NOT WAR

SQUEEZE THE FREEZE WITH THIS ROUSING MASH-UP OF BIG, FAT, SUNNY FLAVOURS

Inside scoop

USED IN

MISS WHIPLASH

PG 116

THE SAVOY CHILL
EARL GREY SORBETTO

THE MEETING AT THE SAVOY HOTEL WAS A BLEND OF DISTINCTIVE FLAVOURS AND THE SCENT OF A WOMAN WHO INDUCED MORE THAN A LITTLE 'HOO-HA'. I SAT LIKE A NAUGHTY SCHOOLBOY IN THE PRESENCE OF A 'GOLD COMMANDER' FROM SCOTLAND YARD. HER MISSION WAS TO PRISE OUT OF ME ANY FUTURE PLANS FOR GLOBAL DOMINATION. I PLEADED MY INNOCENCE AND TOLD HER I WAS IN THE MIDDLE OF WRITING A BOOK ON THE ICECREAMISTS. TO THIS DAY I CANNOT FIGURE OUT WHY A SENIOR OFFICER INTERROGATING AN ICE CREAM MAN WAS DRESSED LIKE A KISSOGRAM IN A COCKTAIL DRESS AND FISHNET STOCKINGS AT 10.00 IN THE MORNING IN THE SAVOY HOTEL. BEING GRATEFUL SHE DIDN'T ASK IF IT WAS A TRUNCHEON IN MY POCKET, OR IF I WAS JUST PLEASED TO SEE HER, I MADE MY EXCUSES AND DEPARTED, BUT NOT UNTIL I HAD QUAFFED THE LAST OF MY EARL GREY TEA AND GIVEN HER A CHEEKY WINK. WHEN I RETIRED TO THE SANCTUARY OF THE ICECREAMISTS, THEY MADE ME THIS CALMING 'EARLY GREY' SORBETTO IN HONOUR OF THE LADY FROM THE YARD.

· 500ml (17fl oz) boiling water · 125g (4oz) caster sugar· 2 Earl Grey teabags
· zest and juice of 1 lemon · ½ an egg white

1. Pour the water and sugar into a bowl, add the teabags and stir together. Allow to steep for 10 minutes, then add the lemon juice and stir again. Cover and refrigerate, ideally overnight, until thoroughly chilled (at least 4°C).

2. Remove tea bags and pour into an ice cream machine. Churn according to the manufacturer's instructions. If making by hand, see the instructions on page 000. Halfway through, add the egg white.

3. When the churning is completed, use a spoon or spatula to scrape the sorbetto into a freezer-proof container with a lid. Freeze until it reaches the correct scooping texture (at least 2–3 hours).

4. Decorate each portion with a little lemon zest before serving.

THE WHIRL IS NOT ENOUGH

Inside scoop

A METROPOLITAN BLEND OF LIGHT AND DISTINCTIVE BERGAMOT FLAVOUR WITH CITRUS NOTES – PURE GOLD. FOR A 'CHILLY BILLY' SORBETTO, USE LADY GREY TEABAGS INSTEAD. THESE IMPART THE FLAVOUR OF BERGAMOT WITH HINTS OF ORANGE AND LEMON.

DAZED & CONFUSED

BLACKCURRANT & RASPBERRY VODKA SORBETTO

IN 2010 I WAS CHARGED WITH CREATING A CUNNING STUNT FOR A MAJOR ICE CREAM BRAND. WE KIDNAPPED A COACHLOAD OF TOURISTS IN BLACKPOOL, STRAPPED THEM INTO A ROLLER COASTER, GAVE THEM AN ICE CREAM AND CHALLENGED THEM TO EAT IT AT 70 MILES PER HOUR WHILE UPSIDE AT UP TO 3GS. THE EXPERIENCE LEFT THE PARTICIPANTS DAZED AND CONFUSED, AND FOOTAGE OF IT BECAME A VIRAL HIT. WE SANK A COUPLE OF THESE SORBETTOS IN THE AFTERMATH TO CELEBRATE THE PENSIONER WITH THE HEART CONDITION WHO SURVIVED 20 RIDES AND LIVED TO TELL THE TALE. UNLIKE HIS FALSE TEETH.

- 120ml (3¾fl oz) water · 120g (3¾fl oz) caster sugar
- 650g (1¼lb) blackcurrants (or blackberries) · dash of creme de cassis
- slug of raspberry vodka · juice and zest of 1 lemon

1. Pour the water into a saucepan and add the sugar. Place over a low heat, add the blackcurrants and bring to the boil, whisking often, until the sugar dissolves. Reduce the heat and allow to simmer for 10 minutes, until the backcurrants soften, continuing to whisk until the liquid turns into a syrup.

2. Pour the syrup into a heatproof bowl and set aside for about 30 minutes, stirring occasionally, until cooled to room temperature. For more rapid chilling, half-fill a sink with cold water and ice and place the bowl of mixture in it for 20 minutes.

3. Add the creme de cassis, vodka and lemon juice and mix with a stick blender. Sieve the mixture into a bowl, to remove any pulp and seeds leaving a thick rich liquid. Cover and refrigerate, ideally overnight, until thoroughly chilled (at least 4°C).

4. Pour the chilled mixture into an ice cream machine and churn according to the manufacturer's instructions. If making by hand, see the instructions on page 15.

5. When the churning is completed, use a spoon or spatula to scrape the sorbetto into a freezer-proof container with a lid. Freeze until it reaches the correct scooping texture (at least 2–3 hours).

6. Decorate each portion with lemon zest before serving.

PSYCHEDELICKER

HELP THE AGED WITH THIS EUPHORIC HELTER-SKELTER OF BLACKCURRANT AND RASPBERRY FLAVOURS WHISKED FACE-DOWN IN CHILLY BLISS

Inside scoop

BRAINFREEZE
WATERMELON AND VODKA SORBETTO

TURN YOUR MIND TO PULP WITH THIS CUNNING SORBETTO. IN MY YOUTH I DISCOVERED WATERMELON IS A GREAT CONDUCTOR OF ALCOHOL, AND IT BECAME THE TRANSPORT DEVICE OF CHOICE FOR STASHING ILLICIT CONTRABAND – SO OVERT THAT IT'S COVERT. SIMPLY CUT A PLUG IN THE TOP OF THE MELON, WEDGE A VODKA BOTTLE UPSIDE DOWN IN THE PLUG AND LEAVE UNTIL ITS CONTENTS HAVE DISSOLVED INTO THE WATERMELON FLESH. THIS IS A SOFTCORE REINVENTION OF THE HARDCORE METHOD AND IS UTTERLY INTOXICATING. WARNING: OVER-INDULGENCE WILL FREEZE THE PARTS OTHER SORBETTOS FAIL TO REACH AND MAY AFFECT YOUR FACULTIES. ADJUST VODKA CONTENT TO MENTAL STATE.

- 125ml (4fl oz) water • 125g (4oz) caster sugar
- 750g (1½lb) seedless watermelon flesh, chopped • 40ml (1½fl oz) good-quality vodka, chilled
- 1 tbsp lime juice • 1 tbsp lime zest, plus extra to decorate

1. Pour the water into a saucepan and add the sugar. Place over a low heat and bring to the boil, whisking often, until the sugar dissolves. Reduce the heat and allow to simmer for 5 minutes, continuing to whisk until the liquid turns into a syrup.

2. Pour the syrup into a heatproof bowl and set aside for about 30 minutes, stirring occasionally, until cooled to room temperature. For more rapid chilling, half-fill a sink with cold water and ice and place the bowl of mixture in it for 20 minutes. Cover and refrigerate, ideally overnight, until thoroughly chilled (at least 4°C).

3. Add the watermelon, vodka, lime juice and zest into the syrup and mix with a stick blender. Pour the chilled mixture into an ice cream machine and churn according to the manufacturer's instructions. If making by hand, see the instructions on page 000.

4. When the churning is completed, use a spoon or spatula to scrape the sorbetto into a freezer-proof container with a lid. Freeze until it reaches the correct scooping texture (at least 2–3 hours).

5. Decorate each portion with lime zest before serving. For a hardcore alternative, serve with a shot of frozen vodka (see page 000).

THE KETAMINE OF COOL. DECEPTIVELY REFRESHING, WITH A FORNICATING FRUITY FINISH AND AN ANAESTHETIC AFTER-EFFECT. OVER-CONSUMPTION MAY LEAVE USERS IN A VEGETATIVE STATE.

Inside scoop

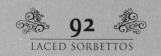
FRISKY BISON

APPLE AND BISON GRASS VODKA SORBETTO

THIS IS AN APPLE SORBETTO WITH A POLISH TWIST. ZUBROWKA IS MY FAVOURITE VODKA AND WAS, UNTIL RECENTLY, BANNED IN THE UNITED STATES BECAUSE IT CONTAINED TINY AMOUNTS OF AN ILLEGAL COMPOUND. IN POLAND ZUBROWKA IS TYPICALLY SERVED CHILLED WITH APPLE JUICE, AND GAINS ITS DISTINCTIVE FLAVOUR FROM BEING MACERATED WITH BUFFALO GRASS (HIEROCHLOE ODORATA) FROM THE BIALOWIEZA FOREST. ACCORDING TO MY POLISH FRIENDS, THIS IS WHERE THE BISON ARE SAID TO URINATE, DEFECATE AND FORNICATE AS THEY ROAM, THEREBY IMBUING THE GRASS WITH ITS COLOURFUL AROMA. THE NAME ZUBROWKA COMES FROM ZUBR, WHICH IS POLISH FOR THE WISENT OR EUROPEAN WOOD BISON.

· 150ml (5fl oz) water · 150g (5oz) caster sugar · 250ml (8fl oz) pressed apple juice, chilled ·
· juice of ½ a lemon · small slug of Zubrowka vodka, chilled ·

1. Pour the water into a saucepan and add the sugar. Place over a low heat and bring to the boil, whisking often, until the sugar dissolves. Reduce the heat and allow to simmer for 5 minutes, continuing to whisk until the liquid turns into a syrup.

2. Pour the syrup into a heatproof bowl and set aside for about 30 minutes, stirring occasionally, until cooled to room temperature. For more rapid chilling, half-fill a sink with cold water and ice and place the bowl of mixture in it for 20 minutes.

3. Add the apple and lemon juices and mix with a stick blender. Cover and refrigerate, ideally overnight, until thoroughly chilled (at least 4°C).

4. Add the vodka, then pour the chilled mixture into an ice cream machine and churn according to the manufacturer's instructions. If making by hand, see the instructions on page 000.

5. When the churning is completed, use a spoon or spatula to scrape the sorbetto into a freezer-proof container with a lid. Freeze until it reaches the correct scooping texture (at least 2–3 hours).

SWEETLY PRESSED APPLE OFFSET WITH THE FRAGRANT HERBAL NOTES. YOU WILL EMERGE FROM THE WOODS FEELING PURGED AND PURIFIED AFTER THIS LITTLE NUMBER.

Inside scoop

LENIN AND LIME

GIN AND TONIC SORBETTO

GREETINGS, COMRADE. THIS QUASI-REVOLUTIONARY SORBETTO IS SO BONE-CHILLINGLY GOOD THAT THERE'LL NEVER NEED TO BE ANOTHER COLD WAR. IT'S ONE OF THE FLAVOURS WE WERE DEVELOPING FOR OUR 'DICTATORS OF COOL' COLLECTION, WHICH INCLUDED OUR OLD FAVOURITES ADOLF HITLER (THE GREAT LICKTATOR), COLONEL GADDAFI (CONE EL GADDAFI) AND DAVID CAMERON (FAKE 99).

• 150ml (5fl oz) water • 150g (5oz) caster sugar • 150ml (5fl oz) tonic water
• ¾ tbsp gin • zest and juice of 1 lime, plus extra to decorate • juice of ½ lemon

1. Pour the water into a saucepan and add the sugar. Place over a low heat and bring to the boil, whisking often, until the sugar dissolves. Reduce the heat and allow to simmer for 5 minutes, continuing to whisk until the liquid turns into a syrup.

2. Pour the syrup into a heatproof bowl and set aside for about 30 minutes, stirring occasionally, until cooled to room temperature. For more rapid chilling, half-fill a sink with cold water and ice and place the bowl of mixture in it for 20 minutes. Pour the tonic water into a bowl, add the sugar syrup, then cover and refrigerate, ideally overnight, until thoroughly chilled (at least 4°C).

3. Add the gin, lime juice and lemon juice to the chilled mixture, then pour into an ice cream machine and churn according to the manufacturer's instructions. If making by hand, see the instructions on page 000.

4. When the churning is completed, use a spoon or spatula to scrape the sorbetto into a freezer-proof container with a lid. Freeze until it reaches the correct scooping texture (at least 2–3 hours).

5. Decorate each portion with lime slices and serve.

YOU CANNOT DEFEAT A NATION THAT ENJOYS ICE CREAM IN MINUS 40 DEGREES. WINSTON CHURCHILL, ON A TRIP TO RUSSIA

THIS BITTER-SWEET SORBETTO HAS SOFT BOTANICAL NOTES AND IS FUEL-INJECTED
WITH ENOUGH ALCOHOL FOR A KICK IN THE BOLSHEVIKS

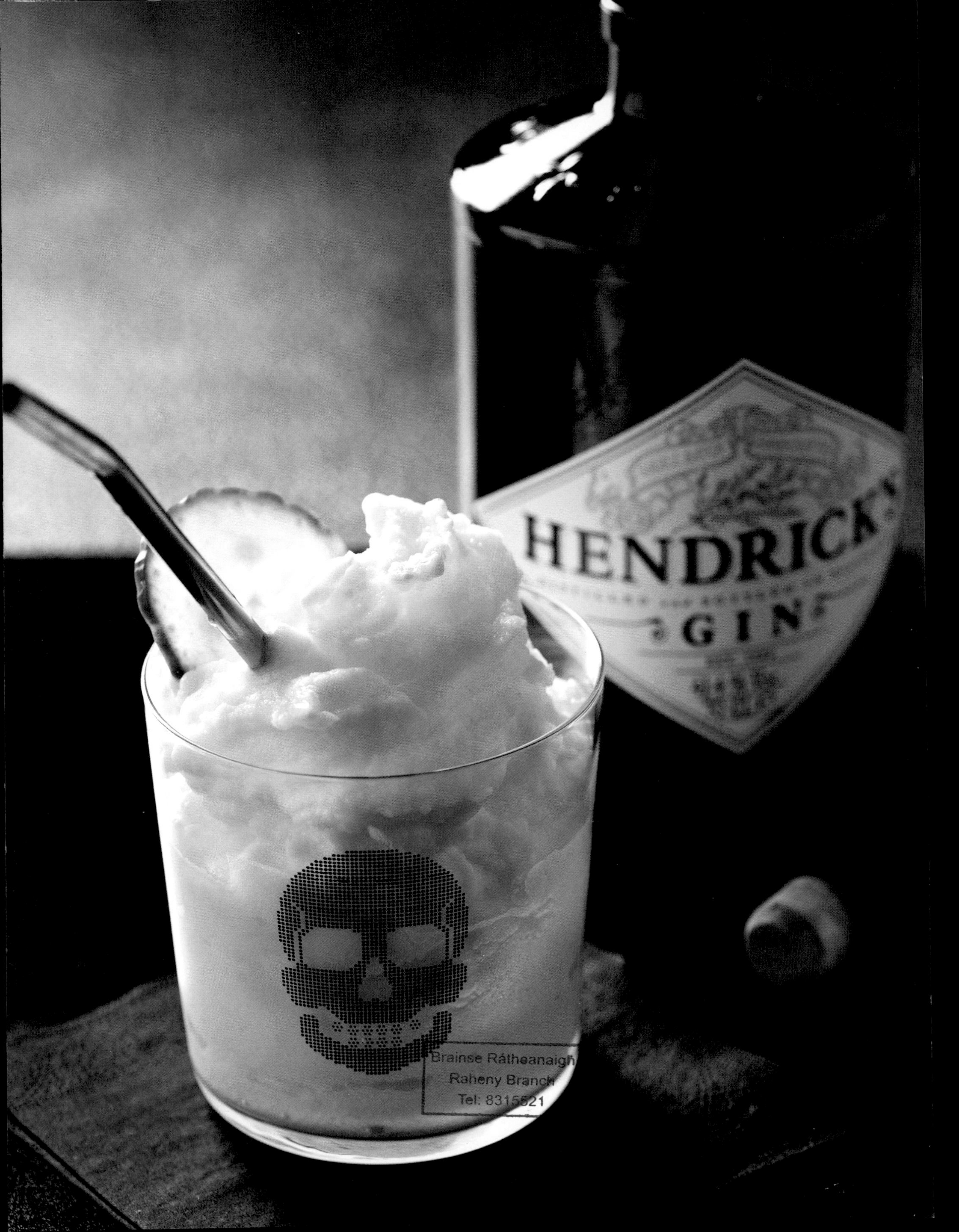
HENDRICK
GIN

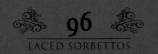
NATURAL BORN CHILLER
MUSCAT SORBETTO

IF YOU EVER SEE AN IRISH MAN WITH A SUNTAN, IT'S RUST. AND UNLESS THE IRA HAD BEEN ON A RECRUITMENT DRIVE IN BRIXTON BACK IN THE 1990S, IT SEEMED UNLIKELY THEY WOULD HAVE MANY BLACK OPERATIVES WITH A CARIBBEAN ACCENT. I MENTION THIS BECAUSE DURING THE '90S THE ONLY DRIVERS BEING STOPPED AT ROADBLOCKS IN LONDON WERE BLACK PEOPLE. THERE HAD BEEN A SPATE OF SPECTACULAR BOMBINGS IN THE VICINITY OF MY OFFICE IN THE CITY. AND MY DEFAULT MODUS OPERANDI IN THOSE DAYS WAS TO KEEP A STIFF UPPER LIP WITH AN EVEN STIFFER DRINK. ON ONE OCCASION, THE RESTAURANT I WAS DINING IN WAS EVACUATED AND WE WERE ALL DIVERTED TO A HOSTELRY WITH SUBTERRANEAN (AND BOMB-PROOF) FACILITIES, CLINGING DEFIANTLY TO OUR AS-YET-UNOPENED BOTTLE OF MUSCAT.

· 70ml (2¾fl oz) water · 70g (2¾oz) caster sugar · 325g (11oz) grapes, preferably Muscat
· slug of Muscat wine · dash of lemon juice

1. Pour the water into a saucepan and add the sugar. Place over a low heat and bring to the boil, whisking often, until the sugar dissolves. Reduce the heat and allow to simmer for 5 minutes, continuing to whisk until the liquid turns into a syrup.

2. Pour the syrup into a heatproof bowl and set aside for about 30 minutes, stirring occasionally, until cooled to room temperature. For more rapid chilling, half-fill a sink with cold water and ice and place the bowl of mixture in it for 20 minutes.

3. Put the grapes into a bowl and blend with a stick blender. Push through a sieve into a bowl and discard the pips and skins. Pour in the sugar syrup, a splash of Muscat and the lemon juice and blend again. Cover and refrigerate, ideally overnight, until thoroughly chilled (at least 4°C).

4. Pour the chilled mixture into an ice cream machine and churn according to the manufacturer's instructions. If making by hand, see the instructions on page 000.

5. When the churning is completed, use a spoon or spatula to scrape the sorbetto into a freezer-proof container with a lid. Freeze until it reaches the correct scooping texture (at least 2–3 hours).

CALL THE BOMBE SQUAD

A PRONOUNCED SWEET, FLORAL FLAVOUR WITH A SUBTLE TART FINISH

Inside scoop

CHE GEGUAVA

SWEET GUAVA SORBETTO

THE SCREAM OF ICE CREAM WAS ALWAYS INTENDED TO BE A COLD FUSION OF POP CULTURE, A PASTICHE ON THE CULTURE OF ADDICTION AND A POLITICAL AND SATIRICAL MELTING POT OF CONTROVERSY. ONE OF THE FORMATIVE CONVERSATIONS I HAD ABOUT THE CONCEPT WAS WITH DEBORAH ROSS, A JOURNALIST FROM THE INDEPENDENT, WHO INTERVIEWED ME ONCE ABOUT MY POLITICAL ACTIVISM. SHE WROTE, 'HE SAYS THAT IN AN IDEAL WORLD HE WOULD COMBINE DEVELOPING ICE CREAM FLAVOURS WITH BEING A REVOLUTIONARY. WE THINK OF REVOLUTIONARY ICE CREAM FLAVOURS. LENIN AND LIME? CHE GEGUAVA? GANDHIFLOSS? WE LAUGH. HE HAS A BIG, FAT, GENEROUS LAUGH. HE'S POSSIBLY GOOD COMPANY, IN OTHER CIRCUMSTANCES...' BY OTHER CIRCUMSTANCES, I THINK SHE MEANT WHEN I WASN'T OTHERWISE ENGAGED IN POLITICAL SUBVERSION.

- 150ml (5fl oz) water • 150g (5oz) caster sugar • 200ml (7fl oz) guava juice
- juice and finely grated zest of 1 lemon • slug of chilled white rum
- 1 fresh red chilli, finely chopped, to decorate (optional)

1. Pour the water into a saucepan and add the sugar. Place over a low heat and bring to the boil, whisking often, until the sugar dissolves. Reduce the heat and allow to simmer for 5 minutes, continuing to whisk until the liquid turns into a syrup.

2. Pour the syrup into a heatproof bowl and set aside for about 30 minutes, stirring occasionally, until cooled to room temperature. For more rapid chilling, half-fill a sink with cold water and ice and place the bowl of mixture in it for 20 minutes.

3. Pour the guava juice into the syrup, mix with a stick blender, then stir in 1 teaspoon of the lemon zest. Cover and refrigerate, ideally overnight, until thoroughly chilled (at least 4°C).

4. Add the rum to the chilled mixture, then pour into an ice cream machine and churn according to the manufacturer's instructions. If making by hand, see the instructions on page 15.

5. When the churning is completed, use a spoon or spatula to scrape the sorbetto into a freezer-proof container with a lid. Freeze until it reaches the correct scooping texture (at least 2–3 hours).

6. Decorate each portion with the remaining lemon zest before serving. For extra Cuban spice, sprinkle a finely chopped fresh red chilli over the ice cream, if you like.

THE GREAT LICKTATOR

AN EXCEPTIONALLY AROMATIC AND MUSKY FLAVOUR, WITH A LONG, SWEET FINISH, LIKE ANY SUCCESSFUL REVOLUTION. POWER TO THE PEOPLE!

Inside scoop

BRAINWASH
OLD ENGLISH CIDER SORBETTO

I HAVE A LONG AND BRUISING HISTORY WITH CIDER, HAVING SPENT MUCH OF MY ADOLESCENCE MARINATING UNDER THE INFLUENCE OF A FERMENTED APPLE OR TWO. IT CAME TO A HEAD DURING A BROOMBALL MATCH ON THE ICE RINK AT BROADGATE CIRCLE IN THE CITY OF LONDON IN 1998. BROOMBALL INVOLVES BANGING A COOKING APPLE-SIZED BALL AROUND AN ICE RINK WITH A TRIANGULAR-HEADED STICK, WEARING RUBBER-SOLED SHOES. WHILE COMPETING TEAMS WENT ABOUT THEIR PREPARATION WITH OLYMPIC RIGOUR, MY LATE BUSINESS PARTNER PETER DECIDED OUR JADED TEAM WAS IN NEED OF A PERFORMANCE-ENHANCING SUBSTANCE. IN THIS CASE, 10% ABV CLOUDY APPLE CIDER. AFTER THE FIFTH BOTTLE, WE FELT INVINCIBLE. ON THE ICE RINK, HOWEVER, WE WERE VERTICALLY CHALLENGED, AND OUR CONFIDENCE DISSIPATED INTO AN ORGY OF CIDER-INDUCED CARNAGE, RESULTING IN A LIFETIME BAN FROM THE SPORT AND OFFICIALS HARPOONING US FROM THE ICE LIKE BLUBBERING MINKE WHALES.

· **125ml (4fl oz) water** · **125g (4oz) caster sugar** · **300ml (½ pint) cloudy English cider**
· **juice of 1 lemon, plus 1 tsp zest** · **zap of ground cinnamon** · **2 lovely apples, to serve**

1. Pour the water into a saucepan and add the sugar. Place over a low heat and bring to the boil, whisking often, until the sugar dissolves. Reduce the heat and allow to simmer for 5 minutes, continuing to whisk until the liquid turns into a syrup.

2. Pour the syrup into a heatproof bowl and set aside for about 30 minutes, stirring occasionally, until cooled to room temperature. For more rapid chilling, half-fill a sink with cold water and ice and place the bowl of mixture in it for 20 minutes. Cover and refrigerate, ideally overnight, until thoroughly chilled (at least 4°C).

3. Add the cider, lemon juice and cinnamon to the syrup and mix with a stick blender. Pour into an ice cream machine and churn according to the manufacturer's instructions. If making by hand, see the instructions on page 15.

4. When the churning is completed, use a spoon or spatula to scrape the sorbetto into a freezer-proof container with a lid. Freeze until it reaches the correct scooping texture (at least 2–3 hours).

5. To serve, cut the apples in half and hollow out with a paring knife. Fill each hollow with sorbetto and decorate with lemon zest before serving.

A FULL-BODIED BLAST OF OLD ENGLAND, WITH TART APPLE FLAVOURS AND A SCRUMPY BITE

Inside scoop

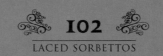
ANY PORT IN A STORM
MULLED WINE AND PORT SORBETTO

COME ALL YE UNFAITHFUL FOR A SEASONAL SORBETTO THAT'S DANGEROUS AT BOTH ENDS AND FRISKY IN THE MIDDLE. THIS LITTLE ELF HAZARD CAME AROUND WHEN WE WERE SCREAMING FOR A BLACK CHRISTMAS WHILST TRYING TO RECRUIT AN ELITE TEAM OF LOLLY-LICKING BLACK DWARVES. APPARENTLY, THERE IS A SHORTAGE OF BLACK DWARVES, WHICH SOUNDS LIKE A TALL STORY INVOLVING SOME SMALL TALK, BUT IN THE END WE WENT WITH PLAN B – A MULLED WINE AND PORT SORBETTO WITH ENOUGH PULLING POWER TO KEEP YOU BUSY UNDER THE MISTLETOE WHILE SOMEBODY PULLS YOUR CRACKER.

· 125ml (4fl oz) water · 125g (4oz) caster sugar · 150ml (5fl oz) red wine
· 1 tbsp ground mixed spice · zap of ground cinnamon and nutmeg
· juice of 1 lemon, plus 1 tsp zest · juice of 1 orange · slug of port

TO SERVE · cinnamon sticks · orange slices

1. Pour the water into a saucepan and add the sugar. Place over a low heat and bring to the boil, whisking often, until the sugar dissolves. Reduce the heat and allow to simmer for 5 minutes, continuing to whisk until the liquid turns into a syrup.

2. Pour the syrup into a heatproof bowl and set aside for about 30 minutes, stirring occasionally, until cooled to room temperature. For more rapid chilling, half-fill a sink with cold water and ice and place the bowl of mixture in it for 20 minutes.

3. Heat the wine, spices, lemon juice and orange juice in a pan and simmer for 5 minutes. Leave to cool for 10 minutes, then add a slug of port. Pour into a bowl, cover and refrigerate, ideally overnight, until thoroughly chilled (at least 4°C).

4. Pour the chilled mixture into an ice cream machine and churn according to the manufacturer's instructions. If making by hand, see the instructions on page 15.

5. When the churning is completed, use a spoon or spatula to scrape the sorbetto into a freezer-proof container with a lid. Freeze until it reaches the correct scooping texture (at least 2–3 hours).

6. Add a cinnamon stick and orange slice to each portion before serving.

Inside scoop FEAR NOT. IF YOUR SPRAY TAN IS FADING, PEC IMPLANTS HAVE LEAKED AND YOUR HALOGEN TEETH HAVE FALLEN OUT, OUR WINTER WHIPLASH IS PUMPED FULL OF ENOUGH FESTIVE FLAVOUR AND WINTER SPICES TO PRESERVE YOU FOR AT LEAST ANOTHER 12 MONTHS

CoCK

TAILS

ARE YOU READY FOR YOUR MEDICATION? LOCK AND LOAD WITH THESE WEAPONS OF MASS SEDUCTION – A DISCOMBOBULATING MIX OF HYPNOTIC PSYCHOTROPICS FOR THE TRULY DEVIANT AND TWISTED. THIS HALLUCINATORY FREEZER CABINET OF NITROGEN-TIPPED VICE CREAM COCKTAILS WILL TRANSPORT CONSENTING PATIENTS TO VERTIGINOUS HEIGHTS OF ORAL GRATIFICATION. REACH FOR YOUR SPOONS AND THEN THE STARS. PLEASE BINGE RESPONSIBLY.

EACH COCKTAIL SERVES 1 (2 SCOOPS, OR HALF A BATCH OF ICE-CREAM FROM THE RELEVANT RECIPE). SCALE UP RECIPES ACCORDINGLY FOR PARTIES.

2 scoops of Sex Bomb ice cream

1 shot of ice-cold absinthe (80% proof minimum)

SERVES: 1 PREPARATION: 5 minutes when the ice cream is already prepared

A DRUGS GIANT BLACKLISTED IT. THE SEX PISTOLS TRIED TO BAN IT AND THE MEXICAN AUTHORITIES IMPOUNDED IT. BOOK YOUR SEAT IN THE BLAST ZONE WITH THE ONE ICE CREAM THE AUTHORITIES COULDN'T DEFUSE, OUR INFAMOUS SEX BOMB ICE CREAM COCKTAIL. THIS ROCKET-PROPELLED ICE CREAM IS LACED WITH NATURAL STIMULANTS (GINKGO BILOBA, ARGININE AND GUARANA) FOR A CARDIOVASCULAR WORK-OUT, OFFSET WITH A MEDICINAL TWIST OF CITRUS ZEST. TOPPED WITH A SHOT OF BURNING ABSINTHE ADMINISTERED STRAIGHT FROM THE BOTTLE FOR EXPLOSIVE RESULTS.

1 Place the ice cream in a martini glass.

2 Freeze the absinthe for at least an hour before serving. Pour the absinthe into a shot glass. Set alight and pour over ice cream.

AN INNOCENT CREAMY MOUTHFEEL WITH A DECEPTIVELY INNOCENT CITRUS INFUSION, FOLLOWED BY AN IMMOBILIZING SHOT OF ABSINTHE THAT'S LIKE BEING HIT IN THE FACE BY A TRANQUILLIZER DART

USES »

SEX BOMB ICE-CREAM

PG 75

Tabasco sauce

chilli flakes

2 scoops of Cold Sweat ice cream

1 fresh red chilli, deseeded and finely chopped

1 tsp finely chopped stem ginger

chilli oil

1 shot of chilled chilli vodka (see below)

SERVES: 1 PREPARATION: 10 minutes when the ice cream is already prepared

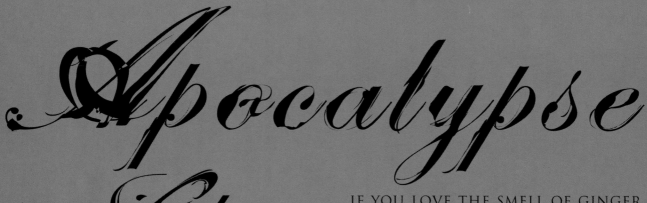

Apocalypse Chow

IF YOU LOVE THE SMELL OF GINGER IN THE MORNING, MELT INTO THIS PARADOX – THE HOTTEST ICE CREAM ON EARTH. MORE INCENDIARY THAN AN AFGHAN FUEL DEPOT, MESSIER THAN A BP OIL SPILL, A FIREBOMB OF CHILLIES, GINGER AND TABASCO SERVED IN A MARTINI GLASS NAPALM-RIMMED WITH TABASCO AND CHILLI FLAKES. FINISHED WITH A SELF-IMMOLATING SHOT OF FLAMING CHILLI VODKA. THIS IS THE ULTIMATE 'SLASH 'N' BURN' ICE CREAM APOCALYPSE GUARANTEED TO PUT HAIRS ON YOUR CHEST – THEN SINGE THEM. BRRRR…

1 Take 2 saucers and drizzle one with Tabasco, the other in chilli flakes. Dip the rim of a martini glass first in the Tabasco, then in the chilli flakes.

2 Place the ice cream in the glass. Decorate with the chopped chilli and ginger, and sprinkle with chilli oil. Serve with a shot of chilli vodka poured over the top and set alight.

Inside scoop A SCORCHED-EARTH INFUSION OF EASTERN HEAT, OFFSET WITH SOOTHING ICE CREAM. TO MAKE YOUR OWN CHILLI VODKA, FILL A BOTTLE OF 80% VODKA WITH WHOLE RED CHILLIES AND LEAVE TO MARINATE FOR A FEW DAYS

USES COLD SWEAT ICE-CREAM PG 73

2 scoops of Vanilla Monologues ice cream

· 25ml (1fl oz) ice-cold Limoncello

50ml (2fl oz) chilled prosecco

2 tsp freshly squeezed lemon juice

SERVES: 1 PREPARATION: 10 minutes when the ice cream is already prepared

The Crybaby

HERE'S OUR SURROGATE ALCOHOLIC INTERPRETATION OF THE STORM IN A D-CUP THAT WAS BABY GAGA. A TITIVATING, ITALIAN-INSPIRED FORMULA OF MADAGASCAN VANILLA PODS AND DOUBLE CREAM CUT THROUGH WITH LEMON ZEST, SPARKLING PROSECCO AND A CHEEKY SPLASH OF LIMONCELLO. SO POTENT, IT WILL LEAVE YOU GURGLING IN A CORNER SLOWLY GOING GAGA.

1 Place the ice cream, Limoncello, prosecco and lemon juice in a bowl and mix with a stick blender blender for 10 seconds.

2 Pour into a champagne saucer and garnish with a raspberry 'nipple' surrounded by lemon zest.

3 Enjoy with a chilled shot of Limoncello for medicinal purposes.

Inside scoop

A DEVIL-MAY-CARE BLIZZARD OF MADAGASCAN VANILLA AND LIMONCELLO CUT THROUGH WITH LEMON ZEST AND SPARKLING FIZZ TO FORM THE PERFECT COCKTAIL

USES >>

VANILLA MONOLGUES ICE-CREAM

FG 21

1 tsp sesame seeds

½ tsp ground cinnamon

2 scoops of Taking the Pistacchio ice cream

dash apricot brandy

dash Italian brandy

SERVES: 1 **PREPARATION:** 10 minutes when the ice cream is already prepared

The Omerta

I ALMOST BECAME BROTHER 'MATT THE MONK' WHEN I WAS INVITED TO JOIN A MONASTERY IN A SOCIAL EXPERIMENT BACK IN 2004. A SUBSEQUENT KICK IN THE CLOISTERS ON ACCOUNT OF MY BAD HABITS MEANT I NEVER GOT AROUND TO TAKING MY VOW OF SILENCE – MUCH TO THE CHAGRIN OF MY COLLEAGUES. HOWEVER, EVEN I WOULD BE REDUCED TO FLAGELLATING MYSELF IN BARBED WIRE UNDERPANTS ON THE FLOOR IF I WERE TO BREAK OUR SICILIAN-INSPIRED OMERTA – A COCKTAIL TO RENDER THE MOST OUTSPOKEN COLD WARRIOR SILENT. RESPECTFUL CONTEMPLATION IS THE ORDER OF THE DAY, AND WHILST WE REMAIN OUTSPOKEN IN OUR DEMANDS FOR WHIRLED PEACE, THIS IS ONE CODE OF SILENCE THAT DESERVES TO BE OBEYED. AT LEAST UNTIL YOU'VE LICKED YOUR GLASS CLEAN.

1 Put the sesame seeds into a small, dry saucepan and shake over the heat until they start to colour. Add the cinnamon and toast together for a few more seconds. Set aside.

2 Place the ice cream in a martini glass and add the brandies. Serve sprinkled with the chopped pistacchios and an additional shot of apicot brandy for those in need of fortification.

A RICH, NUTTY, SICILIAN-INFLUENCED ICE CREAM LACED WITH TWO BRANDIES TO CREATE A SOPHISTICATED COCKTAIL FOR THE BROTHERHOOD OF MAN

Inside scoop

USES »

TAKING THE PISTACCHIO ICE CREAM

2 scoops of Chocwork Orange ice cream

zap of ground cinnamon

1 shot of ice-cold Grand Marnier liqueur

zest of ½ an orange

SERVES: 1 PREPARATION: 10 minutes when the ice cream is already prepared

Fire & Vice

FEEL THE SAND IN YOUR SADDLE AND HOOK UP YOUR CAMEL. THIS ICE CREAM WAS INSPIRED BY A LOST WEEKEND IN THE KALEIDOSCOPIC JAMAA EL FNA MARKETPLACE IN MARRAKECH. A PARADOXICAL CHOCOLATE ICE CREAM COCKTAIL. IT HAS A SUBTLE NORTH AFRICAN INFLUENCE. AFTER DOWNING COPIOUS AMOUNTS OF HOME-BREWED FIG BRANDY WITH MY BERBER GUIDE, THIS CONTRADICTORY IDEA FOR ICE CREAM APPEARED LIKE A MIRAGE...

1 Place the ice cream in a martini glass and dust with cinnamon.

2 Pour the Grand Marnier into a shot glass, flame and pour over the ice cream. Serve decorated with orange zest.

3 Freeze the Grand Marnier for at least an hour beforehand, and enjoy a small glass of it with the ice cream.

Inside scoop

GET YOUR PRAYER MATS OUT FOR THIS INCENDIARY-LACED ELIXIR CONSISTING OF RICH CHOCOLATE GANACHE-STYLE ICE CREAM, ORANGE FLAVOURS, CINNAMON AND FLAMING GRAND MARNIER

USES ➤➤

CHOCWORK ORANGE ICE CREAM

PG 28

- 2 scoops of Glastonberry sorbetto
- 2 shots of ice-cold raspberry vodka
- twist of lemon peel

SERVES: 1 PREPARATION: 10 minutes when the ice cream is already prepared

Miss Whiplash

WE CALL HER MISS WHIPLASH – A ONE-WOMAN GLOBAL WARMING PHENOMENON, DEFROSTING ALL IN HER PATH. HER EPONYMOUS COCKTAIL WILL SEIZE YOU IN A VICE CREAM-LIKE GRIP AND THROW YOU FORWARD AS YOU THROW IT BACK. DELIVERS A MIND ALTERING KICK OF RASPBERRY VODKA TO THE BACK OF THE HEAD, SOFTENED BY SORBETTO. NECK BRACE NOT INCLUDED.

1 Place the sorbetto and vodka in a blender and blend for 10 seconds.

2 Pour into a martini glass and serve with a twist of lemon peel.

Inside scoop

A DEVIANTLY TWISTED SORBETTO COCKTAIL BEATEN INTO SUBMISSION WITH A VERITABLE TORTURE GARDEN OF SEASONAL BERRIES, AND FINISHED OFF WITH A PUNISHING INJECTION OF RASPBERRY VODKA

USES

GLASTONBERRY SORBETTO

PG 83

- Espresso Yourself ice cream

- 25ml (1 fl oz) Amaretto liqueur

- 25ml (1 fl oz) blended whisky

SERVES: 1 PREPARATION: 30–60 minutes when the ice cream is already prepared

The Godfather

FRANK AND PHILIP FREDERICK ARE TWO INIMITABLE ICE CREAM IMPRESARIOS WHOSE LEGENDARY REPUTATION RESULTED IN THEIR BEING DUBBED THE 'GODFATHERS OF COOL'. THIS COCKTAIL WAS INSPIRED BY FRANK'S PENCHANT FOR A GLASS OF SOMETHING MEDICINAL, COMBINED WITH HIS LOVE OF ICE CREAM, AFTER A HARD DAY'S GRAFT. IT'S THE KIND OF COCKTAIL EVEN CRIME FAMILY PATRIARCH DON CORLEONE COULDN'T REFUSE.

1 Spoon the ice cream into an ice cube tray and place in the freezer for an hour, or until hardened.

2 Empty the cubes into a tumbler, add the Amaretto and whisky, then stir and enjoy.

3 Light up a Montecristo cigar, recline in your beaten-up leather wing-back chair and stir the cocktail, slowly watching the ice cream melt into the alcohol.

Inside scoop

INFLUENCED BY ITALY'S CENTURIES-OLD COFFEE CULTURE, THIS HAS RICH, CREAMY COFFEE NOTES SWEPT ALONG TO A SMOOTH AND SMOKY FINISH WITH AMARETTO AND WHISKY

USES »

ESPRESSO YOURSELF ICE CREAM

PG 47

4 egg whites	25ml (1fl oz) ice-cold crème de banane liqueur
200g (7oz) caster sugar	
2 scoops of Carameltdown ice cream	**SERVES:** 1 **PREPARATION:** 10 minutes when the ice cream is already prepared

Molotoffee

IGNITE YOUR REVOLUTIONARY ZEAL WITH THIS INFLAMMATORY MIX OF CHILLED CRÈME DE BANANE LIQUEUR TOPPED WITH DULCE DE LECHE-FLAVOURED ICE CREAM AND INSULATED UNDER A PILLOW OF SOFT MERINGUE BEFORE BEING BLOWTORCHED TO WITHIN AN INCH OF ITS LIFE. THIS BOOZY BANOFFEE BAKED ALASKA IS FLUFFY ON THE OUTSIDE BUT DANGEROUS ON THE INSIDE. IT GROWLS SEDUCTIVELY LIKE A MAMA GRIZZLY WITH A NATURAL GAS PIPELINE BETWEEN HER LEGS. CREATED BY INDEFATIGABLE COCKTAIL MIXOLOGIST ALEX KAMMERLING.

1 Beat the egg whites with an electric whisk until white and fluffy, then slowly whisk in the sugar until you have a stiff and shiny meringue mixture.

2 Place the ice cream in a martini glass and pour the crème de banane over it.

3 Spread a thin layer of meringue over the ice-cream and rim of the glass, then slowly blowtorch the surface until dark brown with a slight crunch.

Inside scoop SATIATE YOUR PYROMANIAC TENDENCIES WITH CARAMEL ICE CREAM DOUSED IN CRÈME DE BANANE LIQUEUR AND COVERED IN THICK MERINGUE BEFORE BEING GENTLY INCINERATED BY BLOWTORCH

USES ≫

CARAMELTDOWN
ICE CREAM

PG 33

ICE QUAKES &/D

SUNDAES

DESSERTS

IT'S OUR PHILOSOPHY AT THE ICECREAMISTS THAT LAWS ARE THERE TO BE BROKEN, RULES ARE THERE TO BE BENT AND EXITS ARE THERE TO BE ENTERED. THEREIN LIES THE SECRET TO OUR MODUS OPERANDI. IN OUR TIME, WE'VE DONE QUESTIONABLE THINGS THAT EXPLORED THE OUTER EXTREMITIES OF THE LAW, GOOD TASTE AND PUBLIC DECENCY WHEN IT COMES TO ICE CREAM. HOWEVER, IN THE COURSE OF OUR RESEARCH WE ALSO STUMBLED ACROSS A CORNUCOPIA OF NATURAL BORN CHILLERS THAT WILL LOWER THE BODY TEMPERATURE OF ANY SELF-RESPECTING ICECREAMIST. SO SCOOP ON DOWN WITH OUR KALEIDOSCOPIC COLLECTION OF IGLOO-ROCKING, ICEQUAKES, KILLER CREAMS AND DESSERT STORMS.

THE RECIPES IN THIS CHAPTER SERVE VARIABLE NUMBERS AND TAKE DIFFERING AMOUNTS OF TIME TO MAKE

VANILLA ICEQUAKE
ICED VANILLA MILKSHAKE

• 300ml (½ pint) ice-cold milk • 3 scoops of Vanilla Monologues ice cream
• ½ tsp vanilla extract (optional)

SERVES: 2   PREPARATION: 5 minutes when the ice cream is already prepared

1 Put the milk and ice cream into a blender and blend together.

2 Taste the mixture, then add the vanilla extract if required. Blend until smooth. Serve in 2 tall glasses with straws.

Inside scoop   PUT THE CHILLA IN VANILLA WITH THIS SEDUCTIVE ICED REFRESHMENT.

USES ≫

VANILLA
MONOLOGUES
ICE CREAM

PG 21

CAFFE ESPRESSO ICEQUAKE
ICED COFFEE MILKSHAKE

• 300ml (½ pint) ice-cold milk • 3 scoops of Espresso Yourself ice cream
2 tsp instant espresso powder or coffee granules, to taste • 6 coffee beans, to decorate

SERVES: 2   PREPARATION: 5 minutes when the ice cream is already prepared

1 Put the milk and ice cream into a blender, add the espresso powder or coffee granules and blend until smooth. Taste, and add more powder or granules if you want a stronger shake.

2 Pour into 2 tall glasses, decorate with the coffee beans and serve with straws.

Inside scoop   A SUPER-CHARGED ICED COFFEE WHIPPED INTO CREAMY BLISS.

USES ≫

ESPRESSO
YOURSELF
ICE-CREAM

PG 47

BERRY ICEQUAKE
ICED BERRY MILKSHAKE

• 300g (10 oz) seasonal berries • 3 scoops Glastonberry sorbetto • 6 blueberries, to serve

SERVES: 2 **PREPARATION:** 5 minutes when the ice cream is already prepared

1 Place the berries in a blender, add the sorbetto and blend until smooth.

2 Pour into 2 glasses and serve with the blueberries on the side.

Inside scoop YOUR DAILY FREEZE OF REFRESHING SUMMER FRUITS

USES ≫

GLASTONBERRY SORBETTO

PG 83

CARAMEL ICEQUAKE
ICED DULCE DE LECHE MILKSHAKE

• 300ml (½ pint) ice-cold milk • 3 scoops of Carameltdown ice cream • ground cinnamon, to dust

SERVES: 2 **PREPARATION:** 5 minutes when the ice cream is already prepared

1 Put the milk and ice cream into a blender and blend until smooth.

2 Pour into 2 tall glasses and dust the surface with cinnamon. Serve with straws.

Inside scoop DULCE DE LECHE-FLAVOURED ICE CREAM WHIPPED INTO A FRENZY OF CARAMEL FLAVOURS

USES ≫

CARAMELTDOWN ICE CREAM

PG 33

STRAWBERRY ICEQUAKE
ICED STRAWBERRY MILKSHAKE

• 225g (7½oz) strawberries, hulled • 300ml (½ pint) ice-cold milk
• 2 scoops of Scarlett Fever ice cream

SERVES: 2 **PREPARATION:** 5 minutes when the ice cream is already prepared

1 Put the strawberries into a blender. Add the milk and ice cream, then blend until smooth.

2 Pour into 2 tall glasses and decorate with a sliced strawberry.

Inside scoop THE PERFECT MATCH FOR THOSE WITH A SUMMERY DISPOSITION: SUPER-COOL STRAWBERRIES AND CREAM

USES ≫

SCARLETT FEVER ICE CREAM

PG 40

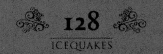
THE JUGGERNAUT
FROZEN HOT CHOCOLATE

OUR CHOCOLATE MELTING POT OF PIPING HOT ENJOYMENT FOR THOSE WHO LIKE TO OVER-INDULGE AT A FURIOUS LICK. WE TYPICALLY DELIVER THIS ONE 'JUGGERNAUT' STYLE – IN GERMAN BEER GLASSES WITH LASHINGS OF WHIPPED CREAM AND A COUPLE OF STRAWS. BY THE END OF ONE OF THESE YOU'LL BE REACHING FOR YOUR STOMACH STAPLER BEFORE LIGHTING A DISTRESS FLARE IN THE DIRECTION OF YOUR NEAREST WEIGHT WATCHERS GROUP.

· 225ml (7½fl oz) milk · 180g (6½oz) milk chocolate, finely chopped, plus extra for curls · ½ tsp ground cinnamon or ginger (optional) · 1 tsp cornflour · 1 scoop of Sex, Drugs and Choc 'n' Roll ice cream · 1 tbsp whipped double cream · chocolate curls, to decorate

SERVES: 2 PREPARATION: 10 minutes when the ice cream is already prepared

1 Warm half the milk in a saucepan over a low heat. Add the chopped chocolate and stir until melted.

2 Whisk in the remaining milk plus the cinnamon or ginger (if using) and cornflour, and heat until the mixture is warmed through. Use a stick blender to mix until smooth.

3 Pour into beer glasses or mugs and top with the ice cream. Add a dollop of whipped cream and some chocolate curls. To make chocolate curls, use a potato peeler or cheese slicer. For extra punch, lace each of the finished quakes with a shot of Irish cream and serve.

LET HELL FREEZE OVER WITH THIS NO-HOLDS-BARRED ELIXIR OF HOT AND COLD CHOCOLATE FLAVOURS THAT WILL STALK YOU RIGHT UP UNTIL YOU COLLAPSE INTO A DIABETIC COMA

Inside scoop

USES » SEX, DRUGS AND CHOC 'N' ROLL ICE CREAM

PG 26

ICEQUAKES

THE ABOMINABULL SNOWMAN

HIGH ENERGY DRINK

DEFROST YOUR INNER YETI WITH OUR INFAMOUS SEX BOMB ICE CREAM LACED WITH NATURAL STIMULANTS (GINKGO BILOBA, ARGININE AND GUARANA) AND A CITRUS INFUSION. FUEL-INJECTED WITH RED BULL AND BITTERS, THIS MONSTER MASH COULD RAISE GODZILLA FROM HIS GRAVE. THE ULTIMATE IN RECREATIONAL MEDICATION FOR THOSE WITH NARCOLEPTIC TENDENCIES. GRRRRRR...

• 2 scoops of Sex Bomb ice cream • 100ml (3½fl oz) Red Bull
• 4 dashes of Spanish or Angostura bitters
• 2 twists of grapefruit, plus finely grated zest (optional)

SERVES: 2 PREPARATION: 5 minutes when the ice cream is already prepared

1 Place the ice cream in a blender. Add the Red Bull and bitters and blend for 10 seconds or until smooth.

2 Pour into a martini glass and serve with a grapefruit twist. Sprinkle with a little grapefruit zest if you wish.

LEMONY SYLLABUB FLAVOUR GIVES WAY TO A CURIOUSLY INVIGORATING COCKTAIL OF RED BULL WITH BITTER NOTES. AN ABOMINABULLY BRILLIANT SUB-ZERO INTERPRETATION OF AN ENERGY DRINK.

USES

SEX BOMB
ICE CREAM

PG 75

RASPBERRY NIPPLE
VANILLA ICE CREAM SUNDAE

HERE'S THE TITIVATING NON-ALCOHOLIC 'FORMULA MIX' OF OUR INFAMOUS BABY GOOGOO COCKTAIL FUSED WITH BOVINE JUICE, CREAM, MADAGASCAN VANILLA PODS, ALMONDS AND JASMINE, THEN CUT WITH LEMON ZEST AND SPICES, SERVED IN A CHAMPAGNE SAUCER WITH A NUTMEG GARNISH AND TOPPED WITH A CHEEKY RASPBERRY NIPPLE.

- 1 scoop of Vanilla Monologues ice cream
- 100ml (3½fl oz) soda water · 2 tsp lemon juice
- 1 tsp Monin orgeat (almond) syrup · 1 tsp Monin jasmine syrup
- 2 dashes of Angostura bitters · 2 tsp ground nutmeg, to dust
- 1 fresh raspberry · 1 tsp finely grated lemon zest

SERVES: 2   PREPARATION: 5 minutes when the ice cream is already prepared

1 Place the ice cream in a blender. Add the soda water, lemon juice, syrups and bitters and blend until absolutely smooth.

2 Pour into a champagne saucer and dust the centre with nutmeg, using a stencil with a 5cm (2in) hole.

3 Top with a raspberry 'nipple' delicately placed in the middle and finish with a pinch of lemon zest.

A HEAVENLY INFUSION OF MADAGASCAN VANILLA, ALMONDS AND JASMINE, VIOLATED WITH A SOPHISTICATED SHOT OF ANGOSTURA BITTERS TO BALANCE OUT THE SWEETNESS IN THIS FRAGRANT ICED DRINK

Inside scoop

USES

VANILLA MONOLOGUES ICE CREAM

PG 21

BABY AFFOGATO

VANILLA ICE CREAM AND COFFEE SUNDAE

AFFOGATO MEANS 'DROWNED', AND WHAT BETTER WAY TO SUBMERGE YOUR SORROWS THAN WITH THIS CLASSIC ITALIAN BLEND OF ICE CREAM AND FRESH ESPRESSO TOPPED WITH COFFEE BEANS? A DEPLORABLY INDULGENT WAY TO IMBIBE STIMULANTS.

• 1 small scoop of Vanilla Monologues ice cream • 1 shot of espresso or strong coffee
• 3 coffee beans, to decorate

SERVES: 2 **PREPARATION:** 5 minutes when the ice cream is already prepared

1 Place the ice cream in an espresso cup and pour a shot of freshly made espresso over the top.

2 Decorate with the coffee beans and serve straight away.

A CLASSIC ITALIAN CONCOCTION OF ANGELIC VANILLA SATURATED WITH ROASTED COFFEE AROMAS. FOR A STRONGER VERSION USE ESPRESSO YOURSELF ICE CREAM (SEE PAGE 47).

USES ≫

VANILLA
MONOLOGUES
ICE CREAM

PG 21

THE
KNICKERBOCKERGLORYHOLE
KNICKERBOCKER GLORY SUNDAE

DITCH YOUR SOCIAL STRAITJACKET – THIS IS CHOCS IN FROCKS ON THE BLOCK! OUR RETRO-COOL CABARET OF CROSS-DRESSING FLAVOURS IS A LASCIVIOUS MIX OF DEVIANT DARK AND WHITE CHOCOLATE ICE CREAMS SANDWICHED TOGETHER IN SEDUCTIVE LAYERS. IT'S PROMISCUOUSLY SERVED STRAIGHT-UP KNICKERBOCKERGLORYHOLE-STYLE, WITH LASHINGS OF HOT CHOCOLATE SAUCE, WHIPPED CREAM AND OTHER NUT-CRACKING PECCADILLOES, TOPPED WITH A STEMMED MARASCHINO CHERRY UNDER A DRIZZLE OF WHITE CRÈME DE CACAO LIQUEUR. SO IMMORAL AND SEXED UP, IT SHOULD BE BANNED UNDER THE OBSCENITY LAWS, LIKE ALL TOP-SHELF THAWNOGRAPHY.

- 100g (3½oz) milk chocolate, finely chopped   • 30g (1¼oz) hazelnuts, roughly chopped
- 1 scoop of Choc and Awe ice cream
- 1 scoop of Sex, Drugs and Choc 'n' Roll ice cream   • whipped double cream
- 1 scoop of Priscilla Cream of the Dessert ice cream   • chocolate curls (see page 128)
- 1 stem maraschino cherry   • slug of white crème de cacao liqueur

SERVES: 2   PREPARATION: 5 minutes when the ice cream is already prepared

1   Make a sauce by melting the chocolate in a heatproof bowl set over a saucepan of gently simmering water, whisking all the time. Pour half of the sauce into the bottom of a knickerbocker glory glass.

2   Now build layers in the following order: chopped hazelnuts, Choc and Awe ice cream, more chocolate sauce, Sex, Drugs and Choc 'n' Roll ice cream, whipped cream, Priscilla Cream of the Dessert ice cream, more whipped cream, chocolate curls.

3   Top the sundae with the maraschino cherry and finish off with a cheeky drizzle of white crème de cacao liqueur.

PRISCILLA QUEEN OF THE DESSERT, CHOC AND AWE, AND SEX, DRUGS AND CHOC 'N' ROLL ICE CREAMS

A NIHILISTIC ORGY OF TRIPLE CHOCOLATE DESTRUCTION BLUDGEONED TOGETHER
IN A KNICKERBOCKER GLORY GLASS FOR YOUR DELECTATION

USES ⟩⟩

PG 22, 23, 26

Inside scoop

NUCLEAR WINTER
WHITE CHOCOLATE ICE CREAM SUNDAE

A THERMONUCLEAR ICE CREAM CONFLICT BETWEEN THE FORCES OF HOT AND COLD ARMED WITH A CLIMATE-CHANGING ARSENAL OF MOUTH-WATERING WEAPONRY. A DESSERT THAT WILL THRILL AND CHILL IN EQUAL MEASURE BEFORE LAUNCHING AN ARSENAL OF CREAMY FRUIT FLAVOURS THAT LITERALLY MELT IN YOUR MOUTH. WE CALL THIS ICE CREAM 'ARMAGEDDON ON A PLATE'. NOW WHERE DID I PUT THOSE LAUNCH CODES...?

- 200g (7oz) mixed seasonal berries (raspberries, blackberries, blueberries, etc.)
- 50g (2oz) white chocolate, finely chopped, plus extra for curls (see page 128)
- 1 tbsp double cream · 1 small scoop of Priscilla Cream of the Dessert ice cream

SERVES: 2 PREPARATION: 1 hour for freezing berries,
plus 5 minutes when the ice cream is already prepared

1 Spread the berries on to a tray and place in the freezer (on 'fast freeze' if you have this setting) for 1 hour, until icy but not completely frozen.

2 When the berries are ready, melt the chocolate in a heatproof bowl set over a saucepan of gently simmering water, whisking all the time. Add the cream and whisk again until blended.

3 Place the frozen berries in 2 glasses or bowls and drizzle the hot chocolate sauce over them. Top with the ice cream and white chocolate curls.

A JUDGEMENT DAY BLEND OF MELTING FROZEN BERRIES JUXTAPOSED WITH PIPING HOT WHITE CHOCOLATE SAUCE AND CRISP, COLD WHITE CHOCOLATE ICE CREAM

USES »

PRISCILLA CREAM OF THE DESSERT ICE CREAM

PG 22

MANTECATO ITALIANO
ITALIAN CREMA ICE CREAM SUNDAE

I HAVE ALWAYS FOUND SOLACE IN THE WORDS OF SKY MASTERSON, MARLON BRANDO'S CHARACTER IN THE FILM GUYS AND DOLLS, WHO SAID, 'AS MY DADDY USED TO SAY, THE ONLY TIME YOU NEED TO BE IN A HURRY IS WHEN THE POLICE ARE COMING UP THE STAIRS.' WHEN I WAS ON THE RUN FROM THE POLICE IN ITALY, EMERGENCY COLD RELIEF APPEARED IN THE FORM OF OUR GELATO MASTER, THE INIMITABLE ROBERTO LOBRANO, WHO WHISKED ME FROM MY HOTEL TO A SMALL RESTAURANT ON THE EDGE OF BOLOGNA AND INTRODUCED ME TO THIS ITALIAN EPIC THAT MOVED AT A GLACIAL SPEED, BEFORE BEING BEATEN INTO SUBMISSION BEFORE MY EYES. THIS ICE CREAM IS SO REVELATORY IN ITS SIMPLICITY THAT I AM INSISTING ON HAVING IT AS MY FINAL MEAL BEFORE THEY PLUG MY CHAIR IN.

- **4 large scoops of The Custardy Suite ice cream**
- **2 tbsp good-quality balsamic vinegar**

SERVES: 2 PREPARATION: 5 minutes when the ice cream is already prepared

I Place the ice cream in a large bowl, add the vinegar and fold together using a spoon or balloon whisk. As the ice cream softens, whisk until the mixture becomes soft and slightly fluffy, like whipped cream. This will take a few minutes.

2 Taste the mixture, adding more vinegar to taste if you wish, then pour gently in folds into 2 glasses. Consume to anything from Puccini's La Boheme…

THE CUSTARDY
SUITE ICE
CREAM

THE GREATEST VERSE OF ITALIAN POETRY EVER WRITTEN. RICH, THICK, EGGY ICE CREAM THAT

SOARS TO VERTIGINOUS NEW HEIGHTS WITH THE HELP OF AN UNEXPECTED

AND UPLIFTING CHORUS OF BALSAMIC VINEGAR.

USES

PG 36

THE FEDERICI

CHOCOLATE AND AMARETTO ICE CREAM SUNDAE

ICE CREAM EVANGELIST ANTONIO FEDERICI FIRST GOT RELIGION WHEN HE CREATED HIS OWN GELATO IN 1896 IN THE MOUNTAINS CLOSE TO THE ITALIAN RIVIERA AND THE HIP RESORTS OF PORTOFINO AND RAPALLO. SINCE THAT EPIPHANY, FAITHFUL DISCIPLES HAVE DEDICATED THEIR LIVES TO SPREADING HIS 'GOSPEL OF COOL' AS THEY HAND OUT SPOONFULS OF FRESHLY MADE ARTISAN GELATO TO THE INFIDELS AND UNCONVERTED. IT HAS SUBSEQUENTLY BECOME THE RELIGION OF CHOICE FOR RECOVERING CATHOLICS AND LAPSED ALCOHOLICS. TO MARK THIS GLOBAL COMMUNION, WE CREATED OUR OWN HOMAGE TO THE MAN HIMSELF WITH A SUNDAE SERVICE YOU CAN TRULY BELIEVE IN. AMEN.

· 50g (2oz) amaretti biscuits · **Amaretto liqueur**
· **2 large scoops of Priscilla Cream of the Dessert ice cream** · **1 sheet edible gold leaf**
FOR THE 'COMMUNION WAFER AND WINE'
· **20g (¾oz) white chocolate** · **4 tbsp Frangelico (hazelnut liqueur)**
· **2 tbsp Amaretto liqueur** · **1 large scoop of Priscilla Cream of the Dessert ice cream**
SERVES: 2   PREPARATION: 10 minutes when the ice cream is already prepared

1 First make the 'communion wafer'. Melt the chocolate in a heatproof bowl set over a pan of gently simmering water, whisking all the time. Using a palette knife, spread the chocolate thinly over a sheet of baking parchment and put in the fridge to harden (about 60 minutes). When set, take a round cutter about 3–5cm (1¼–2in) in diameter, dip it in hot water and cut out 2 chocolate discs. Set aside.

2 Meanwhile, make the 'communion wine' by putting the Frangelico, Amaretto and Priscilla Cream of the Dessert ice cream into a blender and pulsing until the mixture is smooth and creamy. Taste with a teaspoon and adjust as necessary, adding more alcohol if required. Keep in the fridge while doing steps 3 and 4.

3 Put the amaretti biscuits into a bowl and drizzle with the Amaretto liqueur. Set aside.

4 Place both ice creams in another bowl, leave at room temperature for 5 minutes, then gently fold one into the other and mix in the gold leaf.

5 Place the mixture in 2 chalices or glasses and crumble in the moistened biscuits. Top with the chocolate 'communion wafer' and serve with a slug of 'communion wine' alongside.

PRISCILLA CREAM OF THE DESSERT AND CHOC AND AWE, ICE CREAM PG 22, 23

A REVELATORY BLEND OF BITTER-RICH DARK CHOCOLATE, SWEET AMARETTO AND A COMMUNION WINE THAT WILL HAVE YOU QUEUING AT THE ALTAR FOR REFILLS UNTIL JUDGEMENT DAY

Inside scoop

USES ≫

ROCK 'N' ROYAL
VANILLA ICE CREAM SANDWICH

ATTENTION, LOYAL SUBJECTS! HAVEN'T GOT AN INVITE? NOT ON THE GUEST LIST? IT NEVER STOPPED MY LYCRA-LAD ASSOCIATES FROM VISITING THE ROYAL BALCONY AT BUCKINGHAM PALACE FOR AFTERNOON TEA ONE DAY BACK IN 2004. THE ROCK 'N' ROYAL ICE CREAM SANDWICH WAS INSPIRED BY THE MET'S POLICING POLICY AT THE SCOOPING OF THE COLOUR (ONE PROTESTORSANDWICHED BETWEEN TWO COPPERS).

- 1 large scoop of Vanilla Monologues ice cream
- 2 soft chocolate cookies (the softest you can find)

SERVES: 2   **PREPARATION:** 5 minutes when the ice cream is already prepared

1   Press the ice cream face down on one of the cookies and spread evenly with a knife until it reaches the edge. Press the second cookie on top to form a sandwich. If you can't find really soft cookies, make the sandwich with firm ones and put in the freezer for several hours until frozen. Remove and allow to soften for 10 minutes before serving.

2   For maximum effect, use a knife to trim the sandwich into a square shape, then slice into 2 triangles and serve on a plate.

LET THEM EAT KATE, WITH THIS TREASONOUS ICE CREAM SANDWICH FOR THE COMMON PEOPLE THAT IS MOST DEFINITELY NOT BY ROYAL APPOINTMENT. (PLEASE VISIT ME IN THE TOWER WHEN I'M CAUGHT.)

USES ≫

VANILLA
MONOLOGUES
ICE CREAM

PG 21

DEEP-FRIED ICE CREAM
VANILLA ICE CREAM BALLS

AS MY EX-WIFE ONCE SAID, 'SHIT HUSBAND. GREAT COCKTAILS.' AN EPITAPH FOR MY GRAVESTONE IF EVER THERE WAS ONE, AND THIS HISTORIC RECIPE WAS ONE OF HER FAVOURITES. MORE ADDICTIVE THAN CRACK COCAINE AND HOTTER THAN SATAN'S JOCKSTRAP, THESE INCENDIARY BALLS OF FIRE WILL WARM YOUR FROZEN BITS AT 50 PACES.

- 4 small scoops of Vanilla Monologues ice cream • 200g (7oz) digestive biscuits
- 2 eggs • 1 tbsp full-fat milk • sunflower oil, for deep-frying
- icing sugar, to dust • 50g (2oz) Dulce de Leche sauce, warmed (see page 000)

SERVES: 2 **PREPARATION:** 5 minutes when the ice cream is already prepared

1 Line a tray that will fit in your freezer with baking parchment. Quickly roll the ice cream scoops into balls, place on the tray and put in the freezer for 2–4 hours, or until frozen to the touch.

2 Meanwhile, crush the biscuits in a bowl until you have fine crumbs.

3 Remove the ice cream balls from the freezer and quickly roll them in the crumbs, making sure each one is properly coated before freezing again for 1 hour.

4 When the balls are frozen, whisk the eggs and milk together in a bowl. Coat each ball in the egg mixture, shake off any excess, then roll in the crumbs again. Return to the freezer for another hour.

5 Half-fill a large saucepan with sunflower oil and heat until it reaches 200°C (392°F), or a cube of bread dropped into the oil browns in about 30 seconds. When ready, fry two ice cream balls at a time for around 15 seconds, or until golden. Remove with a slotted spoon and roll on kitchen paper to remove any excess oil.

6 Serve immediately, drizzled with the Dulce de Leche sauce and dusted with icing sugar. To spice up the sundae, dust with a little cinnamon.

HOT, CRISP BISCUIT CRUNCH GIVES WAY TO SOFT, COOLING VANILLA ICE CREAM. THIS IS TOP-SHELF THAWNOGRAPHY AT ITS MOST OBSCENE. FIRE-RETARDANT CLOTHING OPTIONAL.

Inside scoop

USES »
VANILLA MONOLOGUES ICE CREAM

PG 21

THE SCOOPERBOWL
CHOCOLATE FONDUE WITH ICE CREAM

SAVE THE WORLD FROM MELTDOWN WITH OUR DOUBLE-DIPPING CAULDRON OF SAUCY SEDUCTION THAT VIOLATES EVERY RULE IN YOUR AVERAGE ICE CREAM MAN'S INSTRUCTION MANUAL.

· 12 scoops ice cream of your choice · 150ml (5fl oz) double cream
· 350g (12oz) dark or milk chocolate, finely chopped · selection of fresh fruit, cut into chunks

SERVES: 2–4 PREPARATION: 2–4 hours for the ice cream balls; 20 minutes for the sauce

1 Line a tray that will fit in your freezer with baking parchment. Quickly roll the ice cream scoops into balls, place on the tray and put in the freezer for 2–4 hours, or until frozen to the touch.

2 When the balls are frozen, warm the cream in a saucepan over a low heat until hot but not boiling. Add the chocolate and whisk until melted. Transfer the sauce to a fondue pot that is heated by a low flame.

3 Arrange the fresh fruit and the ice cream balls on separate plates around the pot. Using a fondue fork, quickly dip the ice cream, then the fruit into the warm sauce and devour immediately.

Inside scoop IT'S ENOUGH TO SEND YOU STIR CRAZY – WAVE AFTER WAVE OF MORALLY HAZARDOUS COCOA FLAVOURS RECLINING IN A SEXUALLY AMBIGUOUS SOCIAL SETTING. NOW WHO'S GOT MY CAR KEYS AND WHERE'S MY WIFE?

ICE Lo

LLIES

I WAS ON A MISSION TO SWEDEN WHEN I INEXPLICABLY FOUND MYSELF ON A SMALL PLANE HEADING TOWARDS THE ARCTIC CIRCLE AND THE WORLD FAMOUS ICE HOTEL. ON ARRIVAL I ATTRACTED CURIOUS STARES FROM OTHER GUESTS ON ACCOUNT OF THE FACT THAT THEY WERE DRESSED TO CHILL IN SKI WEAR, AND I WAS DRESSED TO THRILL IN A BLACK LEATHER TRENCHCOAT AND T SHIRT. GIVEN IT WAS MINUS 40 DEGREES OUTSIDE AND MINUS 5 DEGREES INSIDE, THE ESKIMO AT THE ICE BAR TOLD ME VODKA DIDN'T FREEZE AND WOULD PRESERVE ME SAFELY FOR THE NIGHT AND PRESCRIBED ME ENOUGH ABSOLUT VODKA TO PARALYSE A BABY MAMMOTH. THE TRIP TO SWEDEN NEARLY COST ME MY LIFE, BUT MY LOVE OF ALL THINGS SUB-ZERO HAD BEEN FROZEN IN MY IMAGINATION.

THESE ARE SOME OF OUR HOTTEST LICKS FOR DISCERNING COLD WARRIORS. ENJOY!

YOU CAN ALSO USE OUR SORBETTO MIXES TO FREEZE MORE OF YOUR ASSETS IF YOU WISH.

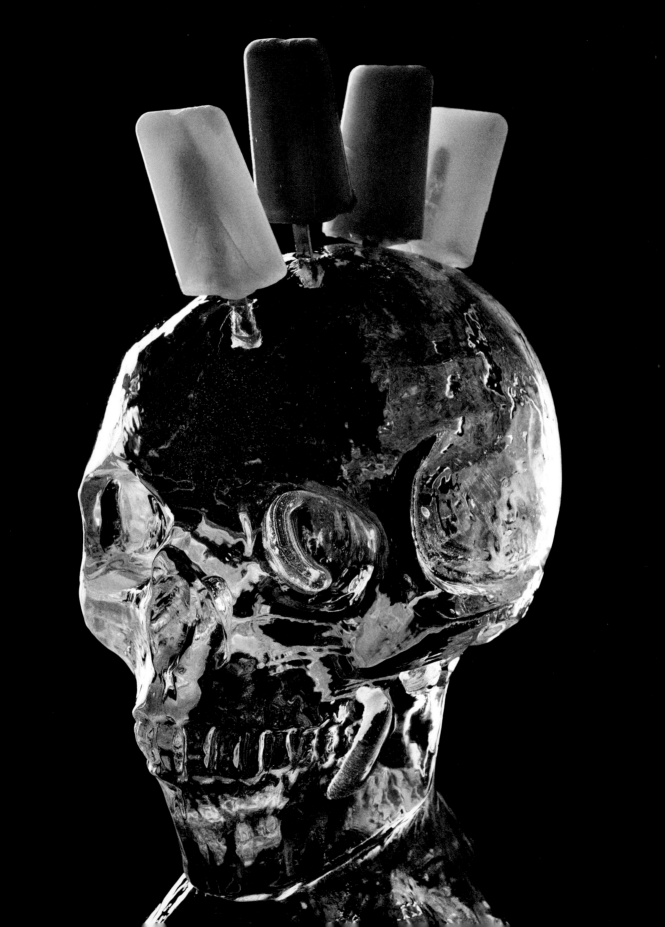

JOHN LEMON

LEMONADE ICE LOLLIES

- 300ml (½ pint) water • 260g (8¼oz) caster sugar
- 200ml (7fl oz) freshly squeezed lemon juice
- dash of lime cordial, to taste

MAKES: 6-8 **PREPARATION:** 10 minutes,
plus about 1 hour freezing

1 Pour the water into a pan and add the sugar. Place over a low heat and bring to the boil, whisking often, until the sugar dissolves. Reduce the heat and allow to simmer for 5 minutes, continuing to whisk until the liquid turns into a syrup. Set aside and allow to cool for 10 minutes.

2 Add the lemon juice and lime cordial to the syrup and whisk together. Pour into lolly moulds, filling them about two-thirds full so that the mixture has room to expand as it freezes. Place in the freezer for about 30 minutes, until almost solid, then insert a stick in each one. Freeze for another 30 minutes.

BABY BRAIN FREEZE

WATERMELON ICE LOLLIES

- 100ml (3½fl oz) water • 100g (3½oz) caster sugar
- flesh from 1 watermelon, seeds discarded
- juice of 1 lime

MAKES: 6-8 **PREPARATION:** 10 minutes,
plus about 1 hour freezing

1 Follow step 1 (above). Put the watermelon flesh in a blender, pulse until crushed, then sieve into a measuring jug. You should have around 500ml (17fl oz) of juice.

2 Add the watermelon juice and lime juice to the syrup and whisk together. Pour into lolly moulds, filling them about two-thirds full so that the mixture has room to expand as it freezes. Place in the freezer for about 30 minutes, until almost solid, then insert a stick in each one. Freeze for another 30 minutes.

AGENT ORANGE

ORANGE ICE LOLLIES

- 240ml (7¾fl oz) water • 240g (7¾oz) caster sugar
- 240ml (7¾fl oz) freshly squeezed orange juice
- dash of ginger cordial, to taste (optional)

MAKES: 6-8 **PREPARATION:** 10 minutes,
plus about 1 hour freezing

1 Follow step 1 (left).

2 Add the orange juice and ginger cordial to the syrup and whisk together. Pour into lolly moulds, filling them about two-thirds full so that the mixture has room to expand as it freezes. Place in the freezer for about 30 minutes, until almost solid, then insert a stick in each one. Freeze for another 30 minutes.

THE PHANTOM RASPBERRY BLOWER

RASPBERRY ICE LOLLIES

- 240ml (7¾fl oz) water • 240g (7¾oz) caster sugar
- 4 punnets of raspberries (about 1kg total weight)
- juice of 1 lemon
- dash of elderflower cordial, to taste (optional)

MAKES: 6-8 **PREPARATION:** 10 minutes,
plus about 1 hour freezing

1 Follow step 1 (above left). Place the raspberries in a blender and pulse until crushed, then sieve into a measuring jug. You should have around 500ml (17fl oz) of juice.

2 Add the raspberry juice, lemon juice and elderflower cordial (if using) to the syrup and whisk together. Pour into lolly moulds, filling them about two-thirds full so that the mixture has room to expand as it freezes. Place in the freezer for about 30 minutes, until almost solid, then insert a stick in each one. Freeze for another 30 minutes.

FIZZ MUST BE LOVE
PINK CHAMPAGNE ICE LOLLIES

THE RESTAURANT RECEIPT READ, '6 X BOTTLES LAURENT PERRIER CUVÉE ROSE BRUT NV CHAMPAGNE, 16 X DOUBLE COGNACS. THANK YOU FOR YOUR CUSTOM, WE HOPE YOU ENJOYED YOUR MEAL.' BACK IN THE HALCYON DAYS OF THE 1990S, LIQUID LUNCHING WASN'T JUST A PASTIME, IT WAS A NATIONAL SPORT FOR THOSE WITH AN APPETITE FOR DESTRUCTION. THANKFULLY, I DON'T DRINK ANY MORE. BUT I DON'T DRINK ANY LESS EITHER. IF WE COULD HAVE STUCK A BOTTLE OF CHAMPAGNE ON A LOLLY STICK, WE WOULD HAVE. INSTEAD, WE HAD TO COMPROMISE WITH A GLASS OF THE PINK STUFF ON A STICK.

· 100ml (3½fl oz) water · 100g (3½oz) caster sugar
· 400ml (14fl oz) pink Champagne (Laurent-Perrier rosé or similar)

MAKES: 6-8 **PREPARATION:** 10 minutes, plus about 1 hour freezing

1 Pour the water into a saucepan and add the sugar. Place over a low heat and bring to the boil, whisking often, until the sugar dissolves. Reduce the heat and allow to simmer for 5 minutes, continuing to whisk until the liquid turns into a syrup. Set aside and allow to cool for 10 minutes.

2 Add the champagne and whisk together. Pour into lolly moulds, filling them about two-thirds full so that the mixture has room to expand as it freezes. Place in the freezer for about 30 minutes, until almost solid, then insert a stick in each one. Freeze for another 30 minutes.

If you can't find pink Champagne, use ordinary Champagne and add a splash of crème de cassis.

I DON'T DRINK WATER. HAVE YOU SEEN THE WAY IT RUSTS PIPES? W. C. FIELDS

A DECADENT KICK OF CHAMPAGNE WITH A SOFT HINT OF FIZZ AND GRAPE AND A SUGARY FINISH

Inside scoop

SHOOT TO CHILL
ABSINTHE ICE LOLLIES

THEY SAY ABSINTHE MAKES THE HEART GROW FONDER. AFTER A COUPLE OF THESE YOU MIGHT GO ABSINTHE WITHOUT LEAVE IN THE NEAREST ASYLUM WITH YOUR FELT-TIPS LIKE VAN GOGH WHO WAS SAID TO PAINT UNDER A BURNING GREEN ABSINTHE HAZE. FEAR NOT, WHATEVER CRIME OR MISDEMEANOUR YOU HAVE COMMITTED, WE ONLY SHOOT TO CHILL WITH OUR SACRED GUN VICE LOLLIES. WE'VE TONED THE ABSINTHE QUOTA DOWN FOR A BETTER-BALANCED LOLLY.

• 600ml (1 pint) water • 100g (3½oz) caster sugar
• 100ml (3½fl oz) Midori (melon liqueur) • 50ml (2fl oz) absinthe, or to taste
MAKES: 6-8 **PREPARATION:** 10 minutes, plus about 1 hour freezing

1 Pour 100ml (3½fl oz) of the water into a saucepan and add the sugar. Place over a low heat and bring to the boil, whisking often, until the sugar dissolves. Reduce the heat and allow to simmer for 5 minutes, continuing to whisk until the liquid turns into a syrup. Set aside and allow to cool for 10 minutes.

2 Add the remaining water, the Midori and absinthe to the syrup and whisk together. Pour into lolly moulds, filling them about two-thirds full so that the mixture has room to expand as it freezes. Place in the freezer for about 30 minutes, until almost solid, then insert a stick in each one. Freeze for another 30 minutes.

For a more potent effect, reduce the amount of water you add to the syrup.

WELCOME TO LOLLYWOOD

Inside scoop FOR THOSE LESS ROMANTICALLY INCLINED, IT WILL ALSO DELAY THE ONSET OF RIGOR MORTIS, PROVIDING AN ADRENALINE SHOT OF THE MIRACULOUS AND THE MEDICINAL WITH ANISEED AND WORMWOOD FLAVOURS FINISHED WITH A SWEET, LOVING LICK OF MELON

SOMETHING SAUCY

CHOC 'N' ROLL SAUCE
DARK CHOCOLATE SAUCE

THIS MELTING POT OF CHOC 'N' ROLL SAUCE IS POSSESSED BY A SUPERNATURAL POWER THAT COULD HEAL THE SICK, RAISE THE DEAD AND LEAVE TONGUES FIRMLY EMBEDDED IN THE CHEEKS OF THE BEAUTIFUL AND THE DAMNED.

- 200g (7oz) dark or milk chocolate, finely chopped
- 170ml (scant 6fl oz) full-fat milk
- 2 tbsp double cream • 30g (1¼oz) caster sugar
- 30g (1¼oz) butter, chopped into small pieces

MAKES: 240ml (7¾fl oz) PREPARATION: 5 minutes

1 Melt the chocolate in a heatproof bowl set over a saucepan of gently simmering water, whisking all the time. Remove from the heat and whisk in the milk, cream and sugar. Return to the heat and stir gently for a few seconds. Remove from the heat again and stir in the butter a few pieces at a time until you have a smooth sauce.

2 Sieve and serve immediately with ice cream, or keep warm in a bain-marie until needed. Fuel-inject the sauce if you like with a slug of Grand Marnier, Amaretto or Baileys Irish Cream.

DULCHE DE LECHE SAUCE
CARAMEL SAUCE

HOW NOW BROWN COW? CARAMELIZE YOUR SOUL WITH THIS INTOXICATING SWEET MILK SAUCE FOR INCURABLE LECHE ADDICTS. WHATEVER I OPT FOR IN THE WAY OF STIMULANTS OR NOCTURNAL ACTIVITIES, THIS STICKY SAUCE WILL ALWAYS BE ONE OF MY PRINCIPAL DRUGS OF CHOICE – A TONGUE-TWISTING LICKETY-SPLIT FROM SOUTH OF THE EQUATOR.

- 400g (14oz) can sweetened condensed milk
- sea salt • ground cinnamon (optional)

MAKES: 400g (14oz) PREPARATION: 1 hour and 10 minutes

1 Heat the oven to 200°C/Gas 3. Pour the milk into a small, shallow baking dish and add a little sea salt. Place the dish within a larger dish and fill with enough boiled hot water to reach about halfway up the sides of the small dish. Cover with foil and bake for 1 hour, until browned, checking occasionally and adding more water to the large dish if required.

2 Remove from the oven and allow the small dish to cool for 5 minutes before whisking the contents until smooth. Dust lightly with cinnamon (if using), then serve with ice cream. The sauce will keep for up to 3 days in the refrigerator. To warm, put in a heatproof bowl and flash in a microwave for a few seconds on High, or warm in a bain-marie.

HOLD YOUR BREATH FOR THIS FRENZIED BLAST OF COCOA FLAVOURS DISTILLED INTO A CHOCOLATE SAUCE THAT MAKES *Inside scoop* FOR THE PERFECT HOT TUB FOR ANY OF OUR ICE CREAMS.

SWEET, SIMMERING CARAMEL NOTES PULSATING IN A DELIRIOUSLY STEAMY SAUCE TO *Inside scoop* A SAMBA BEAT

INGREDIENTS & BASIC TOOLS

All of the ingredients in the book come from well-known food retailers, delis or online stores.

Alcohol: The intoxicant of choice for any self-respecting icecreamist, alcohol is a superior carrier of many flavours. It will depress the freezing point of any ice cream or sorbet, resulting in a softer scoop. It has to be used sparingly – over-indulge and the ice cream won't freeze; get it right and you will be transported to new heights of advanced refreshment.

Cream: Always use the best double cream available.

Eggs: Use free-range where possible; the yolks add richness and structure to ice cream. The whites are not used, so save them to make meringues. Separating eggs is easy. Set out two bowls. Crack the centre of an egg gently on the rim of a bowl and use your thumbs to gently prise the shell apart. Move the yolk back and forth between the shell halves, letting the white drip into the bowl below. Place the yolk in the other bowl.

Milk: Use full-fat milk – nothing less is acceptable.

Sugar: Critically, it allows ice cream to be scooped at sub-zero temperatures without it turning into ice. In a sorbetto sugar unleashes a blitzkrieg of riotous fruit flavours to the front of the palate. In general, use caster sugar as it dissolves quickly, enhances flavour, improves texture and lowers the freezing point of ice cream. Occasionally, muscovado sugar, which is deliciously sticky and dark, replaces caster sugar in certain recipes.

Vanilla pods: Use the best you can find, ideally Madagascan, which are easily found in most major food retailers. The pods are slit with a knife and the seeds then scraped into the custard mix so they can infuse their flavour. If you can't source vanilla pods, you could resort to vanilla extract, but use it sparingly to flavour to your satisfaction.

Bowls: Preferably large and one of which is heatproof; plastic bowls are fine for separating and beating the eggs and making and chilling the custard in your fridge.

Chef's knife: 20–25cm (8–10in), for scraping vanilla beans, preparing fruit and chopping other ingredients.

Food thermometer: Preferably digital, to dip into the mixture (not touching the pan) when cooking the base mix.

Fridge/freezer thermometer: For checking that your fridge and freezer are set at the correct temperature. The fridge should be 4°C/39°F and your freezer -18°C/0°F.

Grater: For preparing citrus zest.

Heavy-based saucepan: For making the base mix.

Measuring jug: With clear markings for exact measuring.

Muslin: For straining very fine custard mixes (usually recipes with nuts in).

Plastic containers: You'll need lots of them, at least 1 litre capacity and with lids, for freezing and storing ice cream.

Scales: Preferably digital, for weighing quantities exactly.

Scoop: Whilst we prefer using an Italian-style spatula, you might find it easier to use a scoop, especially once your ice cream has been frozen. I always keep a couple to hand, ready to dip into warm water for a quicker, smoother scoop when guests are around.

Spatula: Silicone and heatproof, the wider the better, to scrape out and serve the ice cream.

Spoons: A wooden spoon is essential for stirring the base mix; you can never have enough teaspoons and tablespoons, especially for tasting the custards and the final product.

Stick blender: Electric and hand held – for mixing ingredients into the custard and for puréeing fruit.

Strainers: One fine, one medium.

Whisk: Electric for beating the eggs and the base mix.

ICE CREAM MACHINES

Countertop Models

Continuous Models

In general these are a relatively small investment for a decent little machine (buy the best you can afford). It comes with a canister of refrigerant that must be kept upright.

The canister must be pre-frozen for 12–24 hours before churning ingredients. The churning mechanism is also a little flimsy and will struggle with heavy mixes. We recommend buying at least two canisters so that you can make more than one ice cream on the same day. If you can't buy the canisters at the time you buy the machine, they are easily available online.

Once you have chilled your base mix (see page 14), these machines will churn great ice creams in about 40–60 minutes.

A continuous compressor-style machine has a built-in refrigeration unit that doesn't need pre-freezing. This allows you to make as many ice creams a day as you like (provided your base mix has been chilled correctly – see page 14). It also makes the ice cream faster and can deal with thicker ice cream mixes, thus giving you greater flexibility. Some machines allow you to remove the lid to add ingredients during churning rather than adding them through a small opening.

The disadvantages are that it's a big-ticket item for your kitchen; it's not small and can be a bit noisy; it must be handled carefully, kept upright and generally allowed to settle for 12 hours after transit. This type of a machine is a serious bit of kit for serious icecreamists.

Onb the plus side the machine will churn great ice creams in 20–60 minutes, depending on how chilled your base mix is and provided the chill switch has been switched on at least 5 minutes before use.

I CAN RESIST EVERYTHING EXCEPT TEMPTATION. OSCAR WILDE

TROUBLE SHOOTING

When making ice cream, it is possible that the process could be affected by a number of different factors. The following are the most common scenarios and the questions that our icereamists sometimes ask themselves.

WHY ISN'T MY ICE CREAM FREEZING?

» Your ingredients are warm. If your ingredients are at room temperature or above, the ambient temperature is too warm, and this can adversely affect your ice cream. Try to make sure all your ingredients are seriously chilled before use.

» Your equipment is warm. Make sure the freezer container has been frozen long enough in the freezer, as well as the plastic box or canister of refrigerant. If it hasn't, then the ice cream won't freeze properly.

» Your ambient temperature is warm. A warm kitchen can also slow down the freezing process in the ice cream machine.

WHY HAS MY ICE CREAM MACHINE STOPPED OR IS STRUGGLING TO CHURN?

» Check your quantities. Adding too much mixture to the machine can slow it down and cause it to stop. If this happens, remove some of the mixture and continue churning.

» Check your mix. Some mixtures are quite rich and heavy, so if the machine slows down or stops, remove some of the mixture.

I DON'T KNOW WHAT'S WRONG AND I'VE TRIED ALL THE ABOVE

» In a worst-case scenario, use plan B: pour the mixture in a freezerproof container with a lid, place in the lowest compartment of your freezer (where it is coldest) and hit the super-freeze button if you have one. Check every few hours, stirring to see if the ice cream is smooth and silky. Plan B, regrettably, does not compensate for power failure.

INDEX

ACKNOWLEDGEMENTS

The anecdotes that accompany the flavours in this book are based on the real-life experiences of the author. Some names have been changed to protect the guilty.

SPECIAL THANKS
To Frank and Philip Frederick, the Godfathers of Cool, for their support, inspiration and commitment.

THE CURATORS OF ORAL GRATIFICATION
An avalanche of thanks to Rebecca Brown, ice cream paramedic, for her assistance whilst working on black ice, to our incomparable wizard of whirls Anthony 'Scooperstar' Orledge, and to our kaleidoscopic kitchen of cool, including Raquel Pereira, Stefano Mercantani and Yankee, gelato master Roberto 'The Jedi' Lobrano, curator of cocktails Alex 'KY' Kammerling, Josef 'Bunga Bunga' Boni and the team from Caterlink, and Nicola Fabbri and his team.

THE COLD WARRIORS OF THE ICECREAMISTS
The following have performed scooperhuman efforts in making this project a reality: Terry 'The Whip-Hand' Haigh, Zach Duncan 'Scooperhero', Diane 'Flake 99' Furness and Neil 'Show Me the Money' Murgatroyd. Our team of Cold Warriors at The Icecreamists, led by the inimitable Steven 'Thin Ice' Waslin, with award-winning support from Graeme and Martina. Heartfelt thanks to the amazing team at Fredericks for their patience and support, especially David 'Top Gear' Taylor, Matt 'Freeze Your Assets' Fulbrook, Ed 'The Sheriff' Jones, the long-suffering Jenny 'Big Bird' Bostock and Anne 'The Abacus' McFarlane.

THE MEN AND WOMEN FROM THE ICE CREAM AGE
Friends who have helped us keep our cool in the face of a global meltdown: our delightful squeeze Victoria 'Baby Gaga' Hiley, Gary Smith and the team at GS Contracts, James 'The Jolly Cream Giant' Herring and the team at Taylor Herring, Najlaa Jabri for the costumes, Terry Murphy at ISA, Reino at The Great Frog, Ed and Tom at Contrast Creative, Will Pretty at Healeys Printers, photographer Jim 'Meltdown' Marks, Richard Wylie and Jason Lumber at HGF, Jennie Stratton at Creative X, Sandro Hinds at HDH, the team at Widenet, Simon Kennedy for the sculptures, Aurelie Bourguet for the Scream of Ice Cream, Colin Dawe at Vision Solutions, the team at Selfridges – Ewan Venters, Andrew Cavanna, Tanya McMullen and Kerry O'Connor. Finally, Beverly Churchill and Jennifer Squire at CAPCO.

THE O'CONNOSSIEURS
The O'Connor clan and other members of the Irish royal family – you melt me with your love: my wife Nadine 'The Ice Queen' O'Connor, Phillippa 'The Philly Freeze' Ball, my youngest son and gift from god Archie 'Too Cool for School' O'Connor, Anne O'Connor, David 'Frozenballs' O'Connor, Elizabeth and Tom Taylor, Wendy and Ian Taylor, and all the family in the kingdom of Kerry, especially Margaret and Noel at the Bank House, Sis Doherty and family in Killarney, and Dan 'Dare' Downing and the Downing clan.

THE GOOD, THE BAD AND THE FROZEN
A hot, sticky handshake for the animal, the vegetable and the criminal who have kindly (and sometimes unwittingly) provided fun, theatre and chills: the Sex Pistols and Lady Gaga for their services to publicity, Simon at Mishcon, Alun Thomas at Davenport Lyons, Tony 'Double Dipper' Heath, Joe Harnett for steering me through the wreckage, Chris 'Cryogenic' Kelly, Dr Nadim 'Mr Whip It Out' Safdar, Andrew 'Shoot to Chill' McAdams, Richard 'Iced T' Castle, Jess 'Licks at the Flicks' Shaughnessy, Jimi Love and The Icecreamists. Finally, my personal security attachment at the Metropolitan Police, my agent Jonny Pegg, Anders Schonnemann for the sumptuous photography in the book, and those enchanting ice maidens at Octopus Publishing – Eleanor 'Lick My Lips' Maxfield, Yasia 'Whiplash' Williams, Caroline 'Scoop' Alberti and Jo 'Sprinkles' Wilson.

MEDICAL SUPPORT TEAM
A special debt of gratitude to my truly diabetical personal physician and pharmaceutical drug dealer Dr Keightly, who defied expert medical opinion by sustaining my life expectancy long enough for me complete this tome. I now donate my body to medical science.

THE FUTURE NEEDS A BIG LICK
Finally, a big thanks to the people of London. It's a swirling, melting pot of love, the ice cream capital of the world and freezer cabinet for The Icecreamists. God save the cream!

WE ARE THE ICECREAMISTS
The Icecreamists welcome fashionistas, recessionistas, bon vivants, raconteurs, troubadours, revolutionaries, disgraced politicians and lonely housewives. Members of the media and law-enforcement community are not allowed on the premises without the prior written permission of the management.

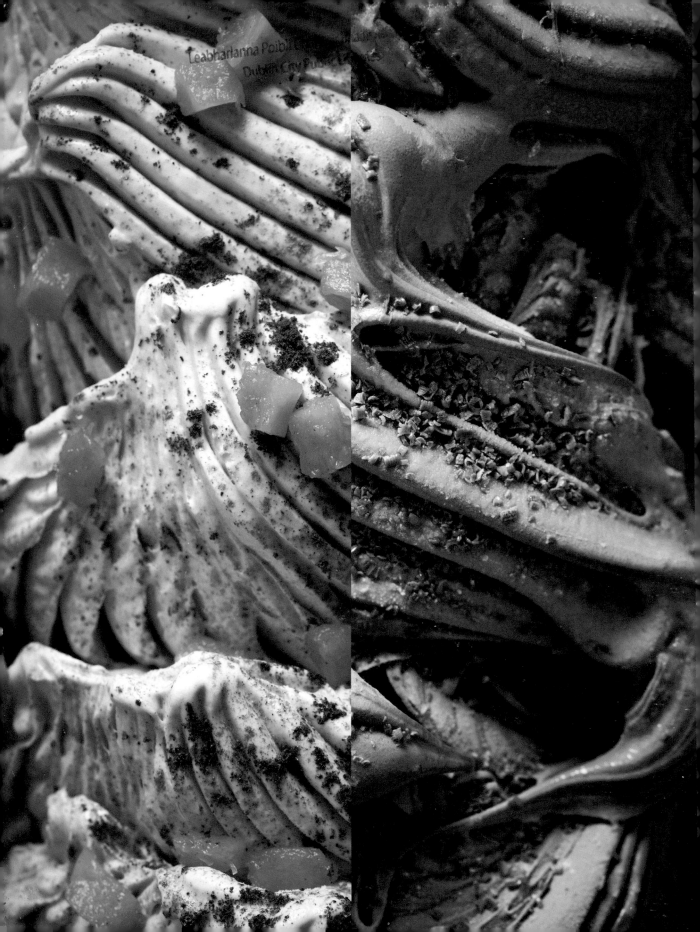